This book is nothing but a series of thoughts begging to be understood. This is an ode to every story never published, love unrequited and word left unspoken. It's words are about recognizing pieces of yourself within other people and finding comfort in that. This is a collection of every time I've sat down to reflect on life and ended up with nothing but an untitled word document. Nevertheless, the words that were once mine, are now yours.

I hope you find what you're looking for.

Yours in Sunshine, Darkness and Every In-between,
Liv Grace

Untitled 17

UNTITLED 17

Untitled 17

All illustrations within these pages were lovingly drawn by Kayla June Southall. Thanks again sunshine. I love you.

Untitled 17

Table of Contents

Untitled 17

Various Letters To Those I Have Loved

Untitled 17

Untitled 17

Dear ____,

You are worthy of love. Stop questioning that. Actually, maybe I should tell you to question it. Question it over and over again until it is finally drilled into your head that someday, somebody will love you with as much love you attempt to put into other people. The pain you experience is nothing short of a heartbreak to witness, but there is no doubt that it is pure. It is a product of your ability to love unconditionally, even when it hurts. I pray that this world and the experiences it brings do not cause you to harden. Keep your edges soft and your heart softer (towards those who deserve it at least). Don't allow your past to hold you back from your future and remember that there is so much life left to live. So many people left to love. So many people who will not reject your love every time it comes their way.

You will find someone. I'm sure of it. Someone who will never make you question yourself. Ever. Someone who will appreciate and accept every single aspect of you, including the ones you don't like. This someone will never make you feel like you have to hold back from loving with everything you have because they will constantly and consistently reciprocate. This love will be a feeling and a choice. No more fading footsteps or slammed doors or nights spent staring at your ceiling, wondering if he would have loved you if you weren't… you. This love will hold no sadness nor remorse nor regret. It will help you to redefine happiness and it is the love you have deserved for so long. A loves that teaches you something new at every chance it gets. A love that reminds you that even when you feel empty, you aren't.

This love will avert its eyes when you eat burgers because it knows you're trying to go vegan. It will kiss you in abandoned gas stations and dimly lit stairwells and everywhere else that most humans don't love. This love will teach you to smile for no reason and that getting out of bed in the morning is a gift you give to yourself everyday. Your past doesn't define you. Neither do your mistakes. It's a new beginning everyday and you can start over whenever you want. You can do anything and sometimes you're going to screw up but I hope you know that you're amazing regardless.

Untitled 17

This love will remind you of that. It will not hurt nor ignore not manipulate. It will be absolutely nothing but love.

As for right now, you need to be patient. This is not a love you can chase after or experience when you choose. It will hit you like a punch in the stomach and leave you breathless in the best way. I know you believe that you love too much. That you feel too much and too deeply because God, you act as if being as brilliantly alive as you are is a bad thing. You are not too alive and you will never be able to teach yourself how to feel less. I think you expect so much from other people because that's what you're willing to give. One day someone will be able to give you the world with no strings attached and no expectation of anything in return. That someone is not "him".

I know right now thinking about him makes you feel dizzy and nauseous and like maybe the answers as to why everything happened the way it did lie at the bottom of red solo cup. They don't. I know that when things between the two of you begin to turn sour again you either eat too much or too little. When you think of the first time he kissed you, you vomit.

He's not worth the stomachache.

All of the places he's touched will no longer ache and the memories you can't seem to forget will eventually be buried in old shoeboxes and dusty photo albums. Every piece of yourself you tore out to give to him will be sewn back into you by others. Before you meet "someone" you will first learn about yourself. You will discover new hobbies and make incredible friends and fall in love with the world, becoming a new person as a result of it all.

Two years from not you won't remember every detail about him. You won't remember what his hair smells like or what brand of cologne he wears. You'll see him in a coffeeshop and feel a flicker of recognition, but nothing else. He will mean nothing to you because you won't be the girl who loved him anymore. You're someone new now. Someone good.

Untitled 17

Someone who plants sunflowers in piles of ashes and takes the path less travelled because she wants the overgrown dirt road to feel appreciated.

One day you will look in the mirror and see everything I see. Someone who is beautiful and funny and intelligent and strong. Someone who is loving and incredible and worthy.

Love deeply, let go gently and live unapologetically.

You will find your "somebody". Be patient. Search within yourself for the person I see. Someone who gives others pieces of herself without thinking of the toll it will take on her. Someone who is left with nothing, yet still makes it out in the end.

I hope you know this about you. You are inspiring and I love you.

Yours Truly,
Olivia

Untitled 17

Dear ____,

I want you to know that you are not a metaphor. You don't exhale stardust or hold the sun in your hands. You were not moulded by God himself, despite the countless nights I was convinced otherwise. I remember thinking that your heartbeat was the product of some divine orchestra. That you were my sole breath of calm in the chaos of this life. But I've seen you crack underneath the pressure of trying to hold up the sky and I sincerely apologize for making you out to be something you're not. Because you are not a Greek God. You are not a prince, nor a saviour, nor a superhero. You are simplicity. You are my smile before bed. My Friday night chick-flick. A place to find comfort and laughter. You are eyes that grew up faster than they should have and hands that are hesitant; scared to reach out again because of how badly you've been hurt before, and that in itself is so inherently, beautifully, human. You are a warm cup of tea and a warm pair of hands and a warm heart that somewhere along the way was convinced that it was cold. You are a horribly sung cover of Hotline Bling and ugly 2 am FaceTime calls and you're the dumbest, stupidest, funniest kid I've ever met in my life. You are my best friend and you are enough. You are more than enough.

I always wrote about you as if you were a metaphor and I suppose I always will because that's how I write about every amazing, unprecedented thing I have ever encountered in my lifetime. Fact is, some people are better than words. They can't be summarized easily, and you my friend proved that point many times.

You ask me to write everything for you because you were never good with words. I always wondered why until I realized you were never the poet, you were the poetry.

Yours Truly,
Olivia

Untitled 17

Dear ____,

Wish me well please. Even if you don't mean it. I need to have some false sense of there being no hard feelings between us. I know there were too many things that have been left unsaid and I'm sorry about that. My heart was pumping weakly and I needed to leave. There's more to life than all of this. There has to be. But for now, all I have (had?) was you and the earth beneath my feet. You're similar in the sense that both of you are constant and kept me standing. I can't explain why I don't want you anymore. I wish I could. I miss when I was still in love with you. I don't know why but this sudden lack of emotion feels suffocating. It's too quiet. My heart is too quiet. It beats, but not as violently as it used to. Why can't I force myself to love you? For the longest time it was just us and the darkness and our mumbled words that constantly meant so much more than what we let on. I need to know that even after all of that, all the love and the trust and the tears and everything, you can still find it in your heart to forgive me. Please. I never begged you for anything but I'll beg you for this in a heartbeat. In a weak, quiet heartbeat but nonetheless, a single beat.

Wish me well.

I'd say I love you, but I don't.

Yours Truly,
Olivia

Untitled 17

Dear ____,

The first time I ever shared my writing with you was when you asked me to read something out loud so you could fall asleep listening to my voice. Many nights after that initial request I read you chapters from books I had lying around. I read our horoscopes, magazine articles and even excerpts from my english text book. I never thought twice about this near daily occurrence until the night I read you something of my own. That night was different. I remember reading "It Came in Waves" to you over the phone, my voice shaking and cracking because I was unsure of what you were going to think. You listened for a solid forty minutes before slowly drifting off to sleep and I honestly felt content with the fact that you had listened at all. I whispered a gentle "goodnight" and you replied with "sweet dreams" as well as a joking remark about how you "didn't really like that one". I remember nodding even though you couldn't see me and hung up the phone.

You didn't call me back and in all honesty I didn't want you to because you would have heard me cry.

In case you were wondering, "that one" was my favourite. "That one" was the first piece of myself I ever really shared with you. That "random chapter from a stupid romance novel" was mine. I wrote it and you didn't like it and fuck, it was supposed to be about us.

You didn't fucking like it and it was written about us.

The next night you asked me to read you your horoscope instead.

I guess that explains a lot.

Yours Truly,
Olivia

Untitled 17

Dear ____,

I want to start this off by saying I'm sorry. I'm sorry for everything I've put you through I'm sorry for hating you and not treating you right. I'm sorry for filling you to the brim with junk and then forcing you to get rid of it. I'm sorry for the burning throat and the tearful eyes. I'm sorry for everything. I shouldn't have starved you, I shouldn't have picked and burned and cut at your skin, I shouldn't have compared you to others and hated you when you didn't look like them. I'm sorry for overworking you and underworking you and holding you hostage in bed despite your pleas for activity. I shouldn't have thrown you against walls, I shouldn't have kept surrendering to the intenseness of the self hatred that came with that. I regret not loving you from the start. You beautiful thing, you oversized thing, you awkward bumbly incredible thing. You will never be a size 0 but you will still be perfect as an 8 or a 10 or a 12 because you're mine. You're all I have and I love you. I love you so much. I spent so much energy loving other people I never took a step back to look at you and Jesus you're perfect. Nobody will ever lust after you you will never be beautiful or envy-worthy to anyone but me. You are everything. You are my home and you are so good to me. You are a thing of stretch marks and cellulite, big hips and uneven breasts. Your gums dip on the left side and one eye crinkles more than the other when you smile and I love it. Your ears are big and your lower jaw juts out and I don't want it any other way because it's you. And you take care of me and keep me standing. Even when I filled you with alcohol and pills and filled your lungs with smoke you still loved me. It's my turn now.

This is my promise to take care of you. To love you regardless of if you're 175 pounds or 130. I promise to exercise you properly and eat good food and allow you to feel loved. Allow people to hug you allow myself to feel the rolls of your belly and the dimples in the back of your thighs and love it anyway. I will change you for the better, I am but what you are now is still beautiful. It always will be. Because its me. I love everybody in this world so much but why did it never occur to me that you were the person who needed my love the most? I never knew I had this inside of me. Inside of you. You are enough. You don't need to look like them because you look like you and thats what I didn't realize until now. Eat and laugh and grow, get sunspots and smile lines and wrinkles show the world that you were here, you felt the sun and that you fucking lived. You lived. You're still living even after my attempts and pleas for you to stop. You kept living. So thank you.

I love you.

I promise to treat you better this time around.

Yours Truly,
Olivia

Untitled 17

Dear ____,

You used to be stained coffee cups, strong arms and stifled giggles as **I** snuck you in through my back door. Now you're mascara stained pillow cases, the smell after it rains and an embrace that no longer feels genuine. You are unrequited thoughts and a once beautiful mind that its not quite there anymore. You are the three short tones of every time you've hung up on me, you are the tightness in my chest after I've sent 6 texts to see where you are and what happened and if you're okay and pleads for you to "pick up your **fucking** phone". You are tear streaked cheeks and lies and broken red string and my blistered pinky toe from the night we walked around for hours and decided we were better off alone. You are the crinkle of the condom wrapper from when we saw each other a week later and all you did the entire time was beg me to have sex.

You didn't see me anymore.

You no longer knew who I was, you saw the vessel that contained me but you didn't know *me* anymore. You used to be mine, you used to **miss** me after two days apart, I used to know you inside and out, but that's gone with the wind, gone with the waves, gone with the notebooks I burned because I couldn't stand reminders of what we used to be. I laid my head on your chest and pressed my ear against your heart and I touched **you** and kissed you and touched you and kissed you and you thought it was because I wanted you (**please** just let me fall asleep on your chest next time) but really I wanted to hear your heart speed up because of me one last time. I knew there would be no next time. I knew there was no fixing this.

You used to be everything but now I don't know if you're even worthy of being something. You are a person who I wish I didn't know because when I look at you I don't remember the heartbreak or the pain or the night I threw up on the side of the road because I was so fucking overwhelmed by how much I loved you, I remember the night I snuck you into my basement and you told me you missed me and the morning you came over and locked our pinkies together and we sat there smiling because we had reached a point where words were no longer necessary. I remember the good morning paragraphs, the I love you's, the sweet dreams', the **come** over's, the times we talked about art and you told me that I was your favourite piece. I see the best in the worst people and it fucks me over because I hold on to those feelings, those good moments, those smiles and I completely disregard the fact that I am emotionally unstable and unhealthy when I look **back** to when you were a part of my life.

You didn't fix me, you were my fix.

I was an addict when I was with you and you put the hero in heroin. They say you're hooked from the first time you use it. You'll never forget your initial high and **I'm** having one hell of a time forgetting about you. I'm **still** stuck in the 'used to be's, my first time and the ecstasy that came with and **in** it but I'm not remembering the bad trips. The times chasing a high hurt me but I'd go back anyway. All of the stupid shit that I've done because of my lust and **love** towards that high. All of the times I'd give it up and feel amazing but somehow end up **with** it again no more than two days later because *I am addicted.*

I recognize that now and I hate the fact that I was addicted to you and our never-ending drama that wore the facade of "love" and I hate you and your lies and I can't wait until the day that **you** finally don't cross my mind.

I can't wait to get clean.

Yours Truly,
Olivia

Untitled 17

Dear _____,

You were the first girl I've ever truly been in love with, and before I get ahead of myself let it be known that I don't regret loving you. I do however have a feeling that you knew all along. Knew about the way I kept dried up contacts from every day I wished to see again (specifically the ones spent touching you). About the way my heart ached to swing from the silver necklace caressing your neck day in and day out. About how I'm drowning in a river I had no idea existed 6 months ago. I miss laughing with you without fighting against every reason we shouldn't be. Being without you feels a lot like rotting from the inside out and no amount of new notebooks or sad songs have been able to numb it. You reached for me in your sleep once. Only once, and ever since I've been practicing how to drop my destiny to be there for you. Once upon a time we were both in-between a rock and a hard place but our friendship was the reason we were able to carve ourselves out.

Maybe that is all we were ever meant to be to each other. Maybe I should have picked your scabs for you. I never wanted you to have to watch yourself bleed. And maybe you ended up hating me for it. And maybe you were the only reason I stayed in the world for the past few months. You loved me but not quite as much as you loved the teeth in your fist or the drugs on the table. My yellow lighter died the other day. The sun sets but I still live 20 minutes away from the water so I guess this whole living thing is meant to be about teaching yourself not to need somewhere - someone - in the first place. I can't keep this ocean in my lungs forever and I know you get seasick anyways but I need to say it. I love you, I love you, I fucking loved you in every sense of the word and I never told you because I began to find comfort in the pistol pressed against my spine. I began to find comfort in the pressure between my vertebrae and the fact you were the one holding the gun. Your hand was so close to my back and in all honesty I would've let you shoot off my every limb if it meant I could spend another minute with your skin on mine. Don't you get it? You'll never stop filling my half empty glass to the brim with something close to love but even closer to anger and I'd kiss your bloody knuckles and listen to you blame the universe for loving everybody but you. I'm sorry I didn't make you feel loved. My therapist told me that it was unhealthy to crave you so badly. Unhealthy to crave the things that couldn't love me back the way I loved them but once I swear she admit she was still in love with her hometown. Theres a metaphor within that if you look close enough. You completely shattered me. The first draft of this letter was written in a car with a beautiful girl who holds my hand and runs her fingers through my hair when I'm upset. Everything was warm, and beautiful and hazy and she looks at me like she's in love with me and I caught myself almost saying it back. But I didn't. Because I don't. Because its you.

It's always going to be you.

Let it be known that while I don't regret loving you, I really I wish I did.

Yours Truly,
Olivia

P.S. I still love you most.

Untitled 17

Dear _____,

This is it. The first "official" piece of writing that will be about you. It feels… good. Different. Unexpected to say the least. Everything that came after meeting you was unexpected, nevertheless amazing. It's impossible to think of a colour you've never seen before and I think that explains why I never thought to expect happiness from somebody like you. You're a colour I've never seen before; something I have yet to figure out. I can't wait for that experience. To be completely honest I don't know much about your soul, nor do I know every single one of your innermost thoughts so I won't pretend to know you inside and out. I don't. But what I do know is that you're afraid of the future. That much is clear to me and I know that the notion of time and tomorrow and next month and next year often overwhelms you and I get that. I'm scared too.

What if the world ends tonight? What if my heart stops beating? What if you step into traffic while you're having a bad day? I know you don't care much for existing. That's okay. I want you to remember that you never have to fake sanity around me. Don't apologize for being off-kilter or for talking about certain things because tomorrow you might walk across the street without looking. Until that car comes I want as much of you as I can get.

Time is too small of a thing to contain people like us and while it's unfortunate that I can never live all the lives I want, I have the privilege of living the life where I let you in. I will eventually let you in. I know admitting that leaves me vulnerable but you're one of the only people I truly trust to never hurt me intentionally. I started to hold back from caring about people and showing emotion but you are the leak in the dam I worked so hard to build and in a sense, you ruined everything because all of these words and feelings are spilling out and there's nothing I can do to stop them. But screw it. Screw time and holding back and dams be damned because with you I feel limitless and I know its simple but you've given me a hand to hold and you've given me new words to write and stories to tell and I don't think I love you (yet) but the way you hold me makes my soul smile. I realize that you're mine and I'm yours and there's no pain or doubt in this and I feel it. I'm not exactly sure what "it" is yet, but it sure as hell is something. If I happen to die tomorrow tell my mom that I love her and my best friend that I meant to text her back and never for one moment question how much meeting you has changed me.

It trips me out when I think of the possibility that time isn't linear, we just experience it as such. Maybe everything happens all at once. Maybe the moment I write this is overlapping with all of the ones I spend kissing you. This moment is when I figure out that I want you to have my heart. This moment is everything and nothing and the beginning and the end and maybe that explains why I feel like I've known you my whole life. Or like I've just discovered you. Or both. This moment is when the car comes. I've spent my whole life saying goodbye and I have to remind myself that whatever it is we have can disappear without warning but fuck it maybe this is the moment that I learn how to hold on. I know we're both trying our best and pretending to be whole but I can't help but wonder if you'd get out of the way. If you hurt, I want you to tell me.

Once you have your license will you drive over the speed limit? What I'm saying is I like holding your hand and I like when you're distracted by the world and I like your eyes and your soul and when you call me baby and trail your fingers across my back and there are so many places I will never go and so many things I will never understand and I don't want your heart to be either. What I'm saying is you're good. You are so good and I want this and us and whatever happens as a result of it. What's I'm saying is I know somedays you want to be reckless but look both ways before you cross the street because whoever you're meant to become will be incredible. They will be successful, intelligent and happy that everything eventually fell into place. Excuse my selfishness, but I want to have the chance to know him.

What I'm saying is I'm here for you, whether you have shit figured out or not. You are so beautiful and lovely and I feel privileged to have the opportunity to love every piece of it.

Untitled 17

So if the car comes, please fucking move.

Yours Truly,
Olivia

Untitled 17

Dear _____,

I never imagined myself writing to you as nothing more than another person I have lost. You're not just another ____ to me. Know that please. I never thought you would be a ____ at all but here we are. I'm sorry things ended the way they did. You already know that but just let me say it one last time, from the bottom of my heart, I'm sorry. I don't really have a place to be writing you something like this anymore but you know me. Knew me… Whatever. The point is, a lot of my words still belong to you and some of them always will. I'm not bitter about that anymore. I know you loved me and I know that when we ended a piece of you died. A piece of me died too but I honestly think it had to. You broke your heart in two trying to love me and gave me the bigger piece in the aftermath so while you're piecing yourself back together again I hope you know that I still hold everything you gave to me sacred and safe. Even when the pieces don't beat anymore. I still struggle with maintaining eye contact and not allowing my voice to shake but I've never struggled with wondering if you truly loved me. We loved each other so damn well and I hope you know that when my future children ask about my first true love I'll tell them about you. I'll tell them about how sometimes people love you when you don't necessarily deserve it. Thank you. It feels weird because you ended up being right. I did end up getting better. I'm on my way to getting better. The storm inside of me still rages but the sky isn't as dark anymore.

I'm laying on my bedroom floor with the window open listening to Patience by the Lumineers on vinyl imagining you in your own room possibly doing the same. Waiting for you to tell me about somebody out there with love in their eyes and daisies in their hair who never mistakes your optimism for naivety. Who never takes you for granted. Who never hurts you the way I did and I hope you find them someday because you deserve that. I hope we both find our someone someday but fuck I am so grateful I was once somebody to you. You are a miracle if I have ever seen one and sometimes I still dream about the world ending and your eyelashes fluttering against my cheek as it crumbles into nothing. Sometimes when everything fades into darkness and ash I still hear your voice telling me "it's gonna be okay, it's gonna be okay, I love you" and I wake up smiling because while you don't love me anymore, there was a point in time when you did. You loved me, and that means something because I can't be all bad if somebody like you loved this terrible mess. I still remember the letter I wrote you for your 16th birthday. How that was the easiest thing I have ever written for anybody and how that revelation made me realize I was about to fall head over heels for you. I was so excited and happy about that. We were younger then, more innocent. You were the grand optimist playing me piano over FaceTime and making gravy before being in bed by 10 and I liked you. I liked you, I liked you then I loved you, I loved you, then I didn't. I'm still not sure which one hurt the most. I didn't allow myself to write about you for a long time because I was afraid it would be exactly like this. Gut instinct. Muscle memory. I'll always remember you, no matter how many times I try to forget. I stopped trying a long time ago.

The summer of two thousand and seventeen was the summer of you. The summer of slushies and pizza and Lil Yachty; hearts beating in sync under the blue sky and your brown eyes staying covered in sunshine.

I'm sorry for asking you to stay. I've been searching for myself my whole life and along the way I found your hands and your heart and your warmth and maybe I'll always be short of breath when somebody mentions your name because you're not just "my ex". You were my window seat, you were the chocolatey bit at the bottom of the drumstick, the fuzzy purple blanket, you were every question and every answer, you were where I found myself and where I lost my words again and again and again and didn't care because it felt so good. You know I never believed in that soulmate, mythological written in the stars bullshit until you. Do you remember the night we were drinking slushies in my grandma's living room and we admit we were soulmates? I am sorry that you got tangled in the nooses I tied around my own neck and I am sorry my own empty lungs stopped you from breathing so often. I'm sorry you couldn't breathe for so long. I see you now and I see us apart and I want you to keep breathing. Forever. Its weird to know you're a stranger to me now. More-so refreshing than anything else. I think a piece of me is always going to love you. I'm always going to love you. Not in the same way, obviously, but you're never going to mean nothing to me.

I always thought highly of how you looked both ways before you crossed the street with me, because you knew I didn't care to. (I do now). I always knew you loved me when you walked on the side closest to traffic, just in case. The car I told you to avoid on your 16th birthday never did end up coming. Not literally at least. I think the toxic pieces of our relationship might have been your car. Maybe I was the car. Nevertheless, thank you for taking my advice. I love you for it.

The cars came and they went and came and went and when one finally came towards you, you moved. I miss you, but I know you're safer on the other side.

Thank you for everything. Time may in fact be linear, but if I had the chance, I would do it all again. A thousand times.

Yours Truly,
Olivia

Untitled 17

Narrations of Loss

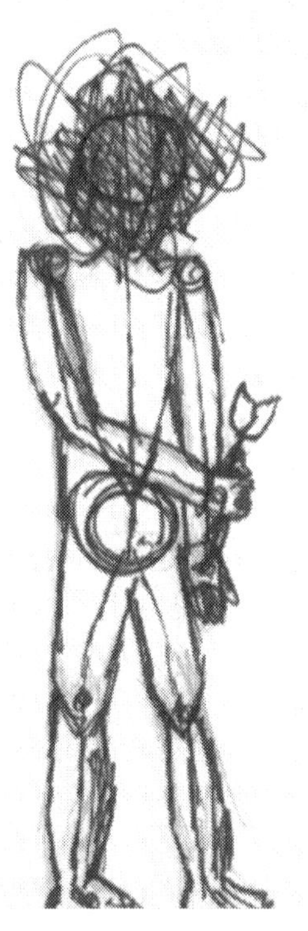

Nothing but a Memory

Loving a memory is hard

Loving a memory means misplaced hands and lips and words

Loving a memory means not caring enough anymore

I had to see you again

I had to feel the warmth of your lips on my neck and your hands on my body

I had to remember you were doing this selfishly

Loving a memory means forgetting voices

It means knowing what you need and not finding it anymore

I didn’t find it

I didn’t see the person I loved when you looked at me that night

I didn’t feel sympathy when you cried

This doesn’t feel right

You’ve become nothing but a cheap game; another breakdown, another poem, line crossed, scream into your chest, another plead for you to love me again

I couldn’t stay who I was when you loved me

I couldn’t be the girl you wanted me to be

Untitled 17

I couldn't stop being pretentious or stop listening to my sad music on Sunday nights or stop writing about you

I couldn't stop wishing we were still a "we" despite everything being pushed into the past and us so desperately pushing at each other because it wasn't us anymore

I feel it all

When I look you in the eyes and cast my own downwards to your mouth

When I don't move

When I don't crave you anymore

I feel safe in my own arms at night

I feel okay without you

Loving a memory means the person you are now is nothing to me

Loving a memory means I'm sorry

Loving a memory means I'm finally okay with this

I'm sorry this is how it ended

I'm also not sorry at all

Thank you for the first love

Thank you for the final goodbye

Thank you for allowing yourself to stay a memory

Untitled 17

August 10th, 2015 - 11:38 pm

Whenever you called I'd be laying in bed, double chin jut out, listening to the sad writing playlist you always used to tease me for. A few hours into the call we'd be screaming Drake at the top of our lungs and my mom would come in to tell me to go to sleep, smiling because she knew I was laughing with you. She'd wish you goodnight and we'd giggle, but for the duration of the call there'd always be music, whether it be from your phone or mine.

Whenever he calls I turn the music off. I'm not loud or giggly because I don't want to be annoying and I know he can't handle that side of me yet. I can't help but wonder if he'll ever be able to. I was reckless and free when it came to you but with him I feel stifled. Suffocated.

Who am I again?

I'm on the phone with him right now, typing this very softly as opposed to how I used to pound away at the keyboard while talking to you. I don't feel like telling him about my writing. I don't feel like telling him that every time I start writing anything about him it ends up being about you.

There is no music. My mom's asleep. I am here and you are not and it is quiet.

Is this what "healing" is supposed to feel like?

It is so quiet.

Untitled 17

"I love you" , "Thanks."

He never says goodnight anymore, only good bye.

The street behind my house has our memories hung between lampposts, drying out like dirty laundry.

There are too many emotions here, lingering from past lives.

I like public transportation and the rain but with him I was always on the receiving end of train wrecks and hurricanes.

Did I love him too much?

Did he not love me enough?

Untitled 17

May 10th, 2017 - 12:09 am

When they asked me where it hurts I pointed to the faded picture of us. I suppose I am here because there are parts of me that won't budge without you. Crosshatched lines of prose littering my skin to hide how deeply I miss the magnificent everything of us.

Your voicemail has become my personal lullaby. Premeditating dreams of dying, just to see if you'd cry. To see if you'd even show up to the funeral.

You used to say I touched the things in thrift stores like I was trying to learn how they ended up where they are. I've begun to touch the photo in my wallet the same way.

Come Home

I've felt like for the last few months of my life the best explanation for everything would be self-inflicted heartache for the sake of my poetry. I'm so caught up in memories and hopes I had so far in the past that I can't remember which ones are relevant in the present. Whenever I talk to you I'm always so tempted to bring up our past, no matter how painful.

Just know that whenever I ask you if you "remember when?" it stands in place of the internalized confession that I can't forget.

Love as Currency

Many ask me if I'm still in love with the muse I used to write about. I've been so confused lately that I flipped a coin to determine this.

Heads I loved you, tails I didn't.

I can't remember anything other than the fact that you were heads and I was tails in terms of what we wanted and what we loved. You expected me to love you unconditionally despite never reciprocating meanwhile I prayed for the day I would wake up to something other than the thought of you.

We were on opposite sides of the same coin. Destined to be a part of each other regardless of the fact our backs were turned. You can't love someone once you've turned your back on everything they're becoming.

You loved my words and I loved yours. Heads and tails. My words came from my mind while yours came from your ass because when I really think about it every word I ever loved was a load of shit.

I can't love you because I don't know you anymore.

I don't know you anymore… thank God for that.

It was tails by the way.

You lose.

Things Change

I think of you differently now.

I don't love you anymore.

I think that should become a given since we haven't truly spoken since last year but anyways, my love is gone. The love I had for you and I'm guessing whatever emotions you felt towards me are gone now too. It feels odd. To not feel anything when somebody mentions your name. Because sometimes I want to cuss you out and joke about you being annoying and joke about all of the times you treated me like garbage but as silly as it sounds I've forgiven you for all of that bullshit. Everything. All of the nights you left me to cry and scream at you over the phone simply because you didn't have the time or energy to deal with my profound emotions. I miss you sometimes, that I cannot deny, but I don't miss loving you. I don’t miss that feeling but I do miss the simplicity of our friendship. The spontaneity of it all. I actually miss that a lot. I don't see you through the same lens anymore, which is naturally what was expected to happen but nevertheless, I miss our friendship. Our 6 hour Facetime conversations. Your 12 am breakfast making, your ugly American Eagle boxers, those stupid thin Oreos you always used to eat. I miss your ever overflowing snack cupboard and your little brother and the comfort that came with being in your presence when I was walking around our neighbourhood, drunk out of my mind. You were somehow always there exactly when I needed you.

I wish we never fell in love with each other. Things would have been so much easier if none of that ever happened. I’m in love with somebody else now and it’s making me believe that maybe I didn’t really love you in the first place. Back then, we were everything. Now all I see when I look at us is one big mess.

I’m sorry for that.

Good Riddance

The night we said goodbye in front of my house I said take care when I really meant come back. I didn't look you in the eyes because the sky was reflected in them and it had never looked prettier. My tongue felt like lead in my mouth and I couldn't bring myself to choke out a last "I love you'. I never told you I missed you because you were never really mine. I was acting like I was fine when really I was having visions of the day I would be minding my own business and see you with someone new. I'm trying to understand that you don't want to love anybody. Like you told me, you just want to be loved.

I want you to know that her words will never fill you like mine.

She will never find a way into your heart like I did.

You will search for me everywhere and wander forever knowing that the comfort my arms used to offer no longer belongs to you.

Cheap lipstick and drunk kisses. A few dates and buckets full of empty words. She will never hold you the way I used to. She will not stay if you hurt her the way you hurt me. She will never write you poetry.

She will never love you like me.

Untitled 17

Throughout the Crests of Every Tree

He became a forest and the harmless seeds of commitment and love that he planted in my heart have grown large. Frighteningly so.

I was waiting for flowers to bloom while trees began to take their place. I can't grow with him anymore. Our roots are tangled and I am trapped. There is no light here.

I can no longer see the sun.

Untitled 17

Lies

So this is what happens when you pretend to have never loved someone after everything has ended. Like maybe pretending every person you kissed after him, was him. It's not fair. It's not fair to you, or to him. Stifling all of these metaphors underneath my palms. Like when your friends curse his name and you wish they would just shut up already. How do you admit you knowingly threw away someone who treated you like the universe personified? Who saw the darkness and loved you for it? I'm cradled in the arms of a boy I don't love back, addressing postcards to you because I truly do wish it were you here instead. How do I stop blaming everything on myself? I'm over you, I promise I am, but the way his torso feels against mine isn't the same and I'm beginning to hate him for it. What happens when he realizes he was nothing but something for me to fuck? My emptiness remains unsatisfied and I doubt it will ever abate because goddammit I am still in love with you. I miss you the way silence misses the low hum of the ceiling fan. It's like when my grandfather had his leg amputated but still felt pain in it when really there was nothing there anymore. Phantom limb syndrome. I survived, but there was less of me. We're still connected, unfortunately. My heart still aches to beat against yours. But these words are too late and my love is too late and just like always, I am not enough.

But trust me, I am over you.

This House

I'm beginning to realize that the house itself never mattered. The worn, antique furniture never mattered and what good are the knick knacks scattered around what used to be our kitchen if there are no longer any memories left to associate with them? It is such an overused cliche but it really does hurt when your home becomes a person and that same person disappears.

I've figured out why I break at the sound of slammed doors and dial tones. It all sounds too much like leaving.

The sunflowers you brought me on the day you left and never came back lay withering on the front mantle for months and I just want to know how somebody who claims to love you can just abandon you like that. Leave somebody once full of light and colour to pale into death and darkness. Regardless of how many times I unplug it, the TV still turns on in the middle of the night, projecting the colours of every sunrise and sunset we spent together across the walls. If we're being quite honest, sometimes I leave it on just to feel something. Anything. Blue sticky tack marks litter the walls from polaroids I can't bear to look at but also can't bring myself to throw away because once the proof of our love is lost, how will I know it ever existed in the first place? When I look at all of the empty wooden picture frames I'm reminded that the boy who once smiled out at me from within them doesn't exist anymore. In all fairness, the girl doesn't either.

Never again will we sit on the kitchen counter top sharing the last piece of garlic bread. Never again will we lay diagonally across the marigold patterned comforter as music from my record player poured into the room. Never again will we binge-watch American Horror story on Friday nights; the blanket we used as a shield against the scary parts is just a purple blanket now. I can't keep living in a house that has pieces of you everywhere. Some days the aching gets so intense that I can clearly hear you playing piano in the basement and happily singing in the shower. I feel so empty when I remember that these are just figments of my imagination now. If these walls could talk they would probably just cry because that's all I've been able to do lately.

I need to leave the place that was once so full of our love but now just echoes every time we screamed profanities at each other. Every time I left and made you feel insane. Every 'I love you' that was said but not meant and honestly by the end of it were barely even convincing. We used to have so much in common that I genuinely did believe that we were made for each other but by the end the only thing we shared was the teal blue refrigerator. In the house with stone walls, creaky floors and warped wooden windowsills, with the peeling flowered wallpaper and the dusty attic filled with your songs and my notebooks we learned how to love despite flaws. We also learned how to hate despite love and the only relief in that is the past tense. You'd have much rather died with more misfortune than regret and I'm curious as to which this house counts as. Have you ever felt homesick in your own home? When I look at the cracked leather chair in the living room I don't see us tangled in each other's arms, watching snowflakes flurry against the front windows, I see you sitting with your head in your hands, spitting your words out like blood as I step out of my body to properly spectate this last memory of us. There is no beautiful triumph this time. We never make up, you never come back and the underdog finally loses. As they often do. The underdog is left in an empty house full of nothing but memories. Nothing but moments touched but never held by you. Nothing lasts forever. The rusty drain pipe will one day be fixed by the next pair of lovers who move in and someday this plane of consciousness will end for good. The very last thought I will ever think will cross my mind and I promise that I love you with the urgency of that moment but it’s time I moved on. It's time I moved out. The windows are open to allow the past to roam freely but I’ve locked every door and thrown away the key. I'm sorry if you come looking because you won't be able to find me this time.

I've come to realize that its much easier to write about us leaving each other then it is to write about us loving each other.

I think that speaks for itself.

Amusement Park

I loved him because he was a merry go round of emotion. Being with him caused me to feel everything a human could possibly feel. He jumpstarted a love, an inspiration I will never be able to escape from. Giving me my passion and taking it back when he left. He didn't leave me with nothing though. In an odd way he left me with everything. The memories, the stories, the high of being so painfully in love with somebody that you would die at their mercy.

The pain of not being able to love him anymore is excruciating. The pain of my promise to stay despite him leaving is excruciating.

I'm still riding the merry go round and I no longer feel love, I feel nauseous.

Strawberry Swing

I can't stop thinking about you and the way you used to look at me. The way I still look at you. The language we spoke through nervous glances and shaky hands and the reality that we were chaos, regardless of how good it felt. We were a disaster waiting to happen. A disaster premeditated without us caring for the consequences.

You became everything to me.

Despite your soft smile and gentle fingertips I became so terrified of that. Soulmates were never a notion I really considered until the day your head landed on my lap and the night your heart landed in my hands. You are green eyes dressed in sunlight. Pink lips dripping with what I initially believed to be strawberries but upon inspection appears to be blood. I never really cared to recognize the difference.

Everything about you was too real. Too certain. I was too certain I wanted to be the one who's love saved you. You said people like us don't get a love like this … like that I should say. Any love between two artists is destined to end in tragedy and in hindsight I should have taken the hint. I guess it just hurts to sit so close to you in silence while words and phrases and past lives play out in our separate minds. That is under the assumption you even think of me at all.

Instead of aching and trembling and touching the way we used to, we stare straight ahead in silence. You desired something real while at the same time remaining terrified of it. I don't think I'll ever understand that.

I look at you and I don't know exactly what I feel anymore, just that I feel too much of it. How is it fair that everyone I love is immortalized in my heart and art forever but to them I was just a fleeting moment? I'm choking on honesty and emotions for you that never seem to stale and strawberries staining my lips red as the rest of me pales into nothingness. You look everywhere but into my eyes and these days watching the clock change is a safer alternative to meeting my gaze. We sit in silence. There

Untitled 17

used to be so much to say but now we barely exchange hello's and every time I try to find the right words nothing comes out.

When the room goes quiet can you hear me screaming your name?

An Ode to Love

This is a poem about love and an ode to the boy who taught me what love is. To put things simply, I loved this boy beyond reason and it drove me insane. I didn’t care. He claimed to love me too which was enough for me due to my bad habit of believing words over actions. He spoke of the love I longed to experience and write about. In hindsight, I should have known better. I always have been a sucker for words.

Real love is not insanity. It is not your heart dropping to your feet every time you see him in public. It is more than lust and bursts of dopamine and struggling to catch your breath when you make eye contact in the hallway. You are experiencing the desperation to feel loved by somebody who doesn't truly love you. I know that some moments are pure. I know he whispers words that make you feel whole and holds you tightly when you're sobbing on the curb outside of your house but he does not love you. Love is not supposed to be crying yourself to sleep every night that he hangs up in anger, it is not screaming and aching and pain and getting high with him just for an excuse to make out. Love is not letting him justify hurting you and touching you when you didn't want him to. Love is not letting him choose when you're worth something and when you're not. You shouldn't have to go to sleep afraid that you’ll wake up to a text that reads along the lines of “we can’t do this anymore” or “last night meant nothing to me” or “sorry. I don’t love you. I was just confused.” It’s not getting felt up under the covers while you know he has a girlfriend and crying in shame after he leaves. It's not fake moans as you pretend to enjoy it. It’s not feeling a lurch in your stomach as he drunkenly slurs that he brought condoms. Somebody who loves you will see more than how hard he's gonna fuck you and you'll get more than a few dick pics at 2am and sentiments about how he’s going to “tear your pussy apart”. Don’t allow me to get too ahead of myself, this is in fact a poem about love and an ode to the boy who taught me what love is.

I am so disgusted by him.

Untitled 17

I don’t want to write about him anymore because it makes me so angry. He makes me so angry please don't say you *ever* loved me because everything you ever did to me proved that point to be false. I was happy before you and I will be happy again even if I have to cut off both of my fucking legs and drag myself to it. So fuck you. Fuck him.

I will bleed out and die before I ever willingly admit to have loved him in the past. I want to be my own muse. I want to overcome this. I want to watch the sunset without feeling the urge to text him about how beautiful it is. This is a story about me now. It is not about him nor for him anymore. I’ve finally stopped hitting snooze on the alarm thats been telling me to let him go already. I woke up, and opened my eyes and maybe I miss him but I don’t need him. I need me more. The me who loves the world fiercely and is at home in her own skin. The me that knows that the truest love I will ever experience will not be explicitly stated. The me that doesn't really like parties or drinking or smoking, the me that he thought was boring but also the me that doesn't care what he thinks. When we said goodbye he sarcastically asked if I was going to say something dramatic and poetic. I was standing there crying and he was laughing as if this were all some big joke. Like he wasn't staring into the eyes of the girl who’s heart he broke.

It hurts.

He made me feel empty and tired and worthless and slapped on the label of love as if that would erase my pain. It never erased it, it stifled it because when I couldn’t give him what he wanted he didn’t care to hear my voice.

I know I am not the only one who feels like this. This is your alarm. If you can relate to this poem, this is your alarm to get whoever you are thinking about out of your life. It hurts. It really does and it took me four years and counting to eradicate him completely but please, listen to me; it’s necessary. I’m not saying it will be easy. It’s hard. It hurts but then suddenly you’re dancing in front of your bathroom mirror with Fergalicious on full blast or you're in the car with your step brother screaming Childish Gambino at the top of your lungs or you're sitting in front of your laptop, writing about the person who completely destroyed you and you don't feel it anymore.

It hurts. It hurts a lot… until it doesn’t.

This is your wakeup call. God only knows I wish I got mine sooner but I’m free now and thats all that matters. I made it. I made it without him.

This is a poem about love and an ode to the boy who taught me what love is. Here’s to you. The boy I gave everything to. The emotionally manipulative, narcissistic, mentally abusive man he will someday become. Thank you for teaching me what love is.

Thank you for teaching me what love is, by showing me exactly what it isn’t.

Unfinished Business

I wonder if you remember the day the sun went out. We had been sleeping soundly, our planet rocking us from within our dreams when I woke up to discover that there was no longer light. You never really knew the difference between having your eyes shut and seeing the pitch black that followed the sun being extinguished.

You kept your eyes closed during those cold few months. I tried to close mine too yet saw no difference in the way your silhouette looked against our bedroom walls. More monstrous than human. It scared me. I scared me. I was confused and felt betrayed by Saturn because a few months back it had made us the promise of a good life together. It was close to the sun and there was warmth and happiness when suddenly everything seemed to be torn away. Everything we had built had been ruined as we forgot to water the plants and cultivate the garden and clean the house. It was too dark. Our plants were wilting. We were wilting.

I know that you continued to reach for me in the dark. I felt your touch, I promise you, I did, but your arms no longer felt like home. Saturn no longer felt like home. We hurt each other unintentionally during those dark days. Tripping over one another and stubbing our toes. I cussed you out because you were always in my way and I felt as if I was always in yours. Things would have been better if we were alone. There would have been less blood. Less bruises. Less hurt. We were stuck with each other though. I am still sorry for that. You should have gone back to earth but you didn’t. You tried to hold my hand because you knew that complete darkness terrified me. I don't think I ever thanked you for that.

Thank you for that.

Empty

I want others to feel something as a result of me because personally I feel nothing. Tell me you fell in love with me, string together lines of poetry about how my skin feels and how my eyes glow in the morning. I'll savour it like all of the sweet things I think but don't say and pack everything up in the event that the memories ever elicit emotion in the future. I said I loved you back because I felt pressured by the love emanating from you and I never wanted to hurt you. I saw it in your eyes and I knew that you knew I would break your heart so you moved on before giving me a chance to un-attach myself. I don't blame you. I wasn't upset by the lack of you so much as the lack of attention and I feel terrible for admitting that but sometimes the truth hurts.

I'm glad I made you feel something.

I'm sorry I felt nothing.

Submissive Nostalgia

I hope you never forget who you were last summer. In writing this I am succumbing to the need to run my tongue across the molars that still taste like extra large cream soda slushies. Falling in love with you multiple times and you knowing, always knowing. Like the way you held me on the couch in your parents living room and allowed me to melt into your arms (I'm sorry I ruined the leather). Let me fall in love with your brown searchable eyes and your kissable lips and distractible fingers coaxing trembling trebles into stuttering staccato's and I still don't know much about music but that sounded poetic didn't it? I still don't know how to hold beautiful things without breaking them but I make the breaking sound poetic. Didn't I? You and I in the backseat of the car, brake lights splashing against your cheeks and my never ending contentment with your hands clasped in mine. The bus stop at Eastgate where you waited and I found you. Every other moment I spent searching for and finding you. Trembling lips and broken elbows I'm sorry I hurt you so badly. I know I told you that you smelt like home but I'd have much rather had you smell like train rides. That would mean you're headed in the opposite direction. Away from me. Us at the playground by your house, legs pumping on swings as we learned how to fly again and me in my deafening screams pleading for you to stop leaving me behind. But god it was beautiful while it lasted. I guess what I'm saying is that I'm beginning to understand why some things just don't work out. I'm not angry or upset, just accepting of the fact that perhaps we were too young to know any better.

I still eat with a small fork and take pictures of flowers growing where they're not supposed to. Some nights I still feel your fearful heartbeats when facing implications of the future. That's to say some things never do change. My favourite colour is orange again. It reminded me of last summer and us and the (beautiful) memories we shared. Summer is coming again and while we may have outgrown each other I hope that you never forget who you were then.

I hope you know that I won't either.

Unloving you

Learning that I didn’t need you in my life to function was more freeing than loving you ever was. You made it seem fashionable to hate the world and I adopted your own cynicism in my futile attempts to love you. You showed me pieces of myself that I never knew nor wanted to know existed. I will never get back the few pieces of myself that you stole and I think that plays a part in what makes me feel whole. I am not who I am today because of you. I am not the desperate, pleading girl I came across as in my poetry. All that I am today, is my doing. The entirety of my love and light has nothing to do with you. While I had never known true beauty until I had loved you, the definition does not correlate with the pain ridden poetry I wrote about us. The definition of love doesn't look like you.

The definition of love looks like me.

Untitled 17

"You Are My Sunshine"

I saw you for what felt like the first time in forever yesterday. Your skin was bathed in neon slices of harsh light and for whatever reason you were still the most beautiful girl I have ever seen. Did you see me? Did you ignore me? I'm not too fond of eye contact or confrontational conversations so I didn't go out of my way to be noticed by you.

You were looking at her like she was the moon and I was digging my fingernails into my thighs. Maybe all I ever wanted to be was something special to you. I burnt myself out trying to become your everything. Your favourite song. Your window seat. Your sunshine. I worked so fucking hard trying to become your sun but you've always lived happier underneath the light of the moon.

I am 150 million miles away from ever being what you want.

Certain Things

Do you remember that song? Certain things by James Arthur? We played it on loop for hours, staring into each other's eyes because everything that was being sung was everything we wanted to say.

"Are you?" you had whispered into my ear, rolling over so that you could look me in the eyes. I nodded, crying, as I usually did when emotions got too strong and I remember you wiping my tears, cradling my head into your chest. I stayed there, eyes closed, listening to your heartbeats pick up and I knew it was coming. I knew it was going to happen. You were certain I was yours and I was certain you were mine and nothing had ever felt so right so I laughed. "What?" you asked, lacing our fingers together and smiling at my wet cheeks and tangled hair. "I think you know what I want to say" I mumbled, certain things still droning on in the background. And that was when you knew too. We cried for hours that night, feeling the intensity true love brought about, knowing nothing of what was to come. Not caring to. Nothing mattered to me that night. Nothing but you.

December 27th, 2016. The first time we said "I love you". The first time I said "I love you" and knew what it felt like to truly mean it. I can't remember the last time you told me you loved me. I can't remember the last time I said it and meant it. It's exactly one year later and Certain Things played on my Apple music. Almost like a sign. A lesson. Evidence that at one point you can mean something more than you ever believed possible and love somebody so much until one year later you are nothing but a shadow to that same person. I miss the passion of it all. I miss being in love. I miss all of the little things that turned into big things and I miss the certainty that I was yours. Certain things don't last forever. Certain things led to us becoming nothing but shadows to each other. Nevertheless, I hope you remember that night.

Remember that I truly (did) mean it.

That I truly (did) love you.

Casualties

You cancelled our plans for the sixth time in a row. I counted. This type of pain is beginning to render me speechless. Nothing feels real anymore. I woke up crying and ate a bowl of Cheerios before throwing them up soon afterwards. I'm still trying to figure out how to live in the absence of you. My mother dropped me off at work and sighed in happiness because it was one of the most beautiful days of summer. I didn't notice. Customers were warm and happy. I received a few newly engaged couples coming in to taste cupcakes for their weddings.

"Hi there how are you?"

"Good, how are you?"

"I'm good, thank you."

I don't feel anything. Somebody messaged me on Twitter today saying that my writing inspired her and made her feel something. She didn't specify what "something" was. People praise my heartbroken bullshit. People claim to love me and while I genuinely do appreciate it, I don't feel it. I broke out in a rash because I took a shower, turning the knob to the highest temperature possible. I didn't notice anything until I started wheezing. I couldn't breathe, yet in a way it felt nice because it was from lack of oxygen not lack of … you. When I scream that I love you it feels so empty. Like I don't mean it anymore.

Why does it seem like all we do is destroy each other?

The Unconfirmed End of O.K.

This poem was supposed to be something entirely different. Narrations of love turns into narrations of loss, as it often happens.

I choked on my tongue the first time I said hello to you. You were and always will be the most beautiful girl I have ever laid eyes on. I'd take a bullet for you, but I'm afraid you wouldn't notice until the sirens come. Some people are just incapable of loving me back and I get it, honestly I do. You loved me at one point but while you loved, I love. You used to feel like home, you know? I'd stand alone and want nothing more than to have you there next to me but some things on this earth aren't worth losing yourself over. I would've done anything for you and I hope you know that. I would've built us a palace on a mountaintop while struggling with your preference for sleeping alone. I'm sorry. I guess the point of this is to say I'm sorry. I'll always love you but it's just painful to constantly feel like you're not enough for somebody. We've proven again and again that sometimes "never" is louder than "always". I never will be enough for you and I'm sorry for that. Thank you for the memories and the laughter but it's just too much right now. I'm headed somewhere different because I deserve love. I deserve somebody who sees more to me than what I can do for them. Don't get me wrong, you loved me well and it was so much fun while it lasted. In the first letter you ever wrote to me you told me I was a work of art. But the thing about that is art was never really your thing. That's okay. Never forget how much you meant to me. I would die for you, and I will continue living for you too. I hope you can do the same.

I choked on my tongue the first time I said hello to you. You were and always will be the most beautiful girl I have ever laid eyes on. But I've always been better at saying goodbye.

Sunday Morning Glory

Or whatever day it was. Tuesday I think? You were staring into me like you had finally found what you were looking for. I had another nightmare about drowning that night. You kissed my forehead, pressing your warm torso against my back and promised I was safe with you. But all good things must come to an end. Some good things were never true in the first place.

This can’t be the end.

You make me feel a lot like my sketches. Messy and unpleasant.

“I don’t want to hurt you anymore”.

But we both knew that it was too late for that. You already broke my heart.

Last night I had a dream that you were drowning with me for once. You tightened your arms around me. Neither living nor dead. Your promises never came.

“There is nothing alive that could stomach the weight of us. Not in this life. Not in the next”.

But it seems impossible to let go of your hand and never reach to grab it ever again.

Familiarity

To the nights you splayed out onto my floral comforter and told me that I was worthy of love. To the nights I began to believe it. We outgrew each other, as it often happens but I hope you never forget who you were then. I hope you know that I won't either.

You gave me love and longing. Reminded me that the story still mattered even when I read the last page first.

The things we did to each other. The things I never apologized for. The things I could never mention once everything was said and done.

I thought I saw you the other day across a crowded room. A quiet remembrance. I don't know if it was you or not.

Didn't care either.

My chest still felt the same.

July

Who were we before it all ended? Before the unsaid goodbye? In-between those sharp breaths while drunkenly searching for constellations? I can't breathe the same anymore. I don't think I've exhaled since August snaked it's fingers around July's throat and told me that every picture was prettier without me.

Long past are the nights we dipped our toes into swimming pools and found each others mouths under the light of the moon. The sky is still dark. Now starless and blank and all-knowing. I could tell you that it hurt but you'd never understand how much.

I lost my best friends and everyone is just telling me to put up a different polaroid. To paint a different picture but I'm still painting us in the forest, the blush of the horizon turning eyes hazel and blue. The three of us running through fields, the soft buzz of passion and friendship and love. The "so much" of love that has since faded.

September has loosened its grip and I know that I'll be okay but I also know I'll never take anything for granted again.

Who were we before it all ended? We were young and careless and in love. We were too naive to ever think there would be an end at all.

Sometimes I wish you'd have at least said goodbye.

"Good Fuck"

Someday I will forget what your laugh sounds like at 2 in the morning. I will forget the rhythm of your chest rising against my back. How we masked our honesty with loud music and cigarette smoke. I will forget everything. Every breathless moment of paths crossed, eyes meeting, fingertips brushing skin and laughter. The goddamn laughter. I think that might be what I'll miss the most.

Someday you'll be nothing but another instalment in narrations of loss.

How much of a person must remain for us to still give them a place in our art? Asking for a … what used to be a, friend.

You can say I came first to you all you want, but according to your friends I was nothing to you but a "good fuck".

In that case I never came at all.

The Night We Met

"I had all and then most of you, some and now none of you". I couldn't stop sobbing when you sent that recording, singing those words, pleading with me to go back to the night we met. I could hear the hurt and all of the pain but more importantly I could hear the love. The endless love that you still have for me regardless of what I did to you. I think that's what hurts the most. You didn't sing that song for me at all, you sung it for who I was in the Dewitt Tim Hortons on that August evening when you spent the whole night trying to make me laugh and I spent the whole night trying not to fall in love with you. It hurts because I know your heart still remembers me as that person. Your heart still remembers and mourns the loss of her, and you still choose to remember me as good. Maybe you do that to deal with your own heartbreak. To deal with mine I pretend that you don't remember me at all. I don't want you to be haunted by the ghost of me. I don't want you to remember me as anything because I know that those memories will ultimately paint me as somebody who hurt you. I hope you don't still think about me because if you do maybe you miss me as much as I miss you and maybe if I kept my arms open for a little while longer you would have come home and maybe I can't deal with all of the maybe's anymore and I just want to know why everything had to happen the way it did. You never came back and it made me feel empty when I realized that I will never see your eyes light up again when they meet mine. I am never going to feel your touch again, I am never going to hear your voice again, I am never going to watch the world pass by next to you again, I am never going to be yours again because I don't deserve to but God it still hurts. Who's supposed to eat the last piece of garlic bread? Who's supposed to notice the flowers growing in the cracks of the sidewalk? Who's supposed to get me a small fork when my mom forgets? Who's supposed to love me the way you did?

I hope if you ever see this you know that I love you and I always will. I hope you have stopped hurting.

I hope you have given up on the girl from the night we met because she doesn't exist anymore.

Untitled 17

Explanation

My writing does not reflect who I am.

It reflects who I once was.

I write about who I've loved but more importantly, about those who completely destroyed me as a result of it.

They are the ones I will never grow tired of writing about.

They showed me the pain of loving unreciprocated, causing me to blossom into something better and stronger than what I initially was.

Somebody who was capable of untangling webs of lies and years of emotional abuse and filling that darkness with light.

My writing reflects all that I have been through.

It reflects the fact that I love.

That despite everything, I am able to love again.

Untitled 17

Narrations of Love

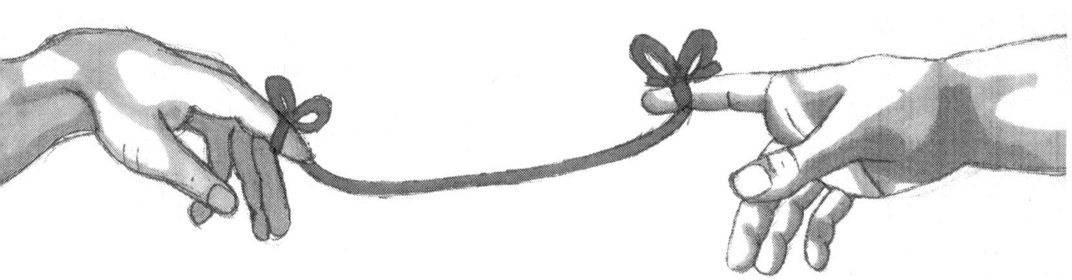

Untitled 17

Live for Me

"Would you die for me?"

I think one of our greatest mistakes as humans is our assumption that every question arises beside a definitive answer. What colour is the sky? Blue? Pink? Purple? Depends when you're looking at it. Sometimes there are multiple answers to seemingly simple questions and yes or no examples such as "Would you die for me?" warrant much more than the anticipated response. I would do absolutely anything for her and I hope she knows that by now, yet at the same time I don't want to burden her with mornings met by my absence. Her bed is no place for my decaying corpse and I doubt she'd choose to reach for my hands once they've turned bloated and blue. We love the stars but there are already countless scattered above our heads. She doesn't need another out there, burning lonely and dim when I'd much rather be by her side. As long as she is on this earth in all of her trust and patience, reclined in my passenger seat I can't imagine being anything less than alive. I don't want her tearing into the earth after I've been lowered into the ground, shedding tears that I can no longer brush away. I don't want the person who has shown me laughter and hope to ever be phased by any thoughts that imply otherwise. What good would I do for her as a pile of ash? Frankly, I would die for anyone if given the chance. Although she reminds me everyday that life can be beautiful. She is so beautiful.

And to answer the question, yes I would die for her. But everyday I choose to live for her instead.

Insanity

I believe to be losing my mind in the best way. Dedicating my words to a broken boy who more often than not renders me speechless. He is so beautiful that it leaves me to wonder what good deed I committed to ever deserve him in the first place.

Does it even matter?

In his arms I am sacred. I've always craved a religion that needed me as much as I need it.

Would you have done any differently?

I melt into wax every time he is near me. I crumble into everything I've ever been afraid of becoming. Not afraid so much as unknowing. I used to not like the unknowing. It was almost as scary as saying I'm halfway in love with him.

Wanna live with me forever within a daydream?

I feel like I've known him my whole life and loved him for longer. Please believe me. I would never lie. Especially not to him.

Simulated

We speak of nothing being real but really, what if this is a dream? Some alien experiment? A simulation? What if everything we do on this earth ends up meaning nothing? I believed that nothing existed until I witnessed the love you hold inside of you. The light, always there, sometimes flickering but never ceasing to burn. Your love is real. You are real and you are so beautiful. You are filled with intelligence and stories. Memories of a childhood gone but never forgotten, filled to the brim with all of the curiosity, love and courage I could ever need. Who cares if the world isn't real or if this life does not matter? We are real and our love is real and that in itself should be enough to convince us of a Greater Something. It is enough.

We are enough.

Untitled 17

2:52 PM

Take me back to November where we met in the backseat and shared the same heart beat. Sunsets photographed on snapchat with power lines underlining everything we wished we could say.

I'll meet you there.

I've loved and I've lost. I've known and I haven't. I was never really sure of anything until I met you. I thought it was all just a waste of time. The grass is always greener somewhere and the sky will get bluer as the days pass.

In all honesty the sky was never my greatest interest when I was with you. There were other things I'd have rather been looking at.

I waited for it and you and your beautiful eyes. Maybe you'll never come back. Maybe you will.

I love you enough to know I'll be okay either way.

Vitriolic Alcoholic

The shattered left knee cap of my old home is a bruise I can't seem to stop pressing. I don't have anything better to do with these hands. I love you in the same way we drink. Without fear for death or consequence. A whiskey stained dream where nobody runs away or dies at the end. To feel the weight of your head on my heart for the rest of eternity would serve to become nothing less than heaven sent. We can plant wildflowers in our wounds and teach each other how to love wild things without connotation of endings. Whatever the antonym of vitriolic is. Whatever Kurt and Courtney could have been. I ask you to come sit next to me the way the desert floor begs the rain to fall.

I would cut my ear off to continue making art about you. I would eat the yellow paint. And the blue. And the purple. So long as you promise to be there to stop me.

How blissful it feels when we want to be rescued and we are.

Dog Days

There are 2 instances in which I clearly remember you quietly closing the car door behind you as I collapsed into sobs and drove away. In the first instance I brought you a big mac, a medium fry and a strawberry Fruitopia. I remember giving you a weak hug outside your front door. Hoping you'd read the note I left in the paper takeout bag and that maybe that would be enough to keep you safe for the night. I wrote more than I meant to. Most of it was simply begging you to stay on this planet with me when I really had no place in this request. Nor any place to ache every time you reminded me that you wished you died in your sleep the night before. That night I told my step brother I was terrified of living a life without you. That night you shut the door behind you and my chest heaved. I went home and I cried and cried and cried. I don't think I ever told you about that because I began to believe that one day I would wake up beside the sun and you wouldn't. Everything got really scary for a while, then one day you came over to my house and I made us vegan avocado pesto sauce. We laughed the way we used to in September. Before we realized how broken everything really was. You smiled with your eyes that night. The night I hopped the curb in the Tim Hortons drive thru because I was too busy singing that the dog days were over. With conviction for once. The night I realized that life was still hard for you, but you continue to live regardless. The night I realized that you felt lucky to be alive, the night I watched you collapse into fits of laughter and I couldn't find the right words to say. I couldn't express my gratitude. You weren't there yet, but you were finally headed in the right direction. "Thank you for making me so happy. I don't wanna jinx anything but I'm happy". You had said this with an overbearing air of nonchalance. As if that exclamation alone didn't change my life. You didn't need to say it, I saw it in your eyes. Happiness was finally coming for you. You shut the door behind you and my chest heaved. I went home and I cried and cried and cried. I don't think I ever told you about that because I believed that one day I would wake up beside the sun and you wouldn't.

I have never felt so thankful to have been proven wrong.

You Are All

It takes a certain type of person to love somebody like me. I am happy that person is you. I am happy we found love on a planet unfit for humans. Ordinary humans, anyway. Just as we admired Saturn for its lopsided rings and deep craters I admire you for your flaws. Every interesting character has many. You are flawed in the sense that earth has so much to offer you, yet you pass up the opportunities because you would rather be with me. Me. Out of all people. Your love has helped me to pick up the pieces. When we sit on those rings and talk to the moon the same way we did on the train tracks near your house, I see you. Underneath all of the noise and the wind and the static, I feel your fingertips tracing I love you's on my back. I hear your voice whispering that I am safe. That I am loved. I feel so loved and I used to hope there was somebody like you meant for me yet when I actually met you I felt taken aback. I was unprepared for you. I didn't know how to love you properly but I think I am beginning to figure it out. I have fallen in love with you a thousand times since we ended up here. Every morning I am first given the choice of looking outside our bedroom window, or into your eyes.

Either way, I am seeing my universe.

Cigarettes and Burrito Bowls

What came first? The flies or the act of flying? This is going nowhere.

You had teased me about eventually writing about this moment. This moment and every other moment. Cigarette in hand, pink blushing my cheeks “yeah right”. I could never grow tired of this. Feeling so incredibly close to somebody that you know there will never be room for regret. We are not two, we are one and I’m pretty certain I’ve loved you since you were born. Probably longer than that. The sun looked over her shoulder to say hello to us that day. Watched you run around the cement staircase and discuss your orbit around me.

What came first? Forgiveness or sin? This is going nowhere.

I think of you farthest from the boundaries of this existence. Like maybe you’ve always been a day dream. A lost thought. An open-ended question. You in your crinkled smiles and loud poetry hiding behind punk rock. You in your black coffee and sarcastic comments about my own soft words. You in your never-ending paradox. I don’t think we’ve ever apologized to each other. What is there to apologize for? I’m sorry for finally finding you? I’m sorry for becoming the person you would eventually love more than life itself?

What came first? The lovers or the love?

It's okay if this is going nowhere, so long as I end up there with you.

Revelation

I remember plunging into the deep end of sin upon meeting her. I remember coming to terms with the reality of my heart. The reality that it loves regardless of who the recipient is. It is hard to feel invalid in your interests when that invalidity is based solely on who you have loved before. It is hard to question who you really are and acknowledge the possibility that you are not who you pretend to be. I aspire to one day love without consequence. Love without explanation. Love for the sake of… loving. Love is simple and it is kind. It is the reason for life. It is also the reason why I often question who I truly am. I can't help but see something wrong with that.

I am coming out… as a person who is capable of large amounts of love.

Someday I will love without drowning.

I will love without feeling obligated to confess.

Apocalypse

The world ended with an awful bang and I was left alone, choking in the pitch darkness on a life I wasn't ready to give up yet. The ringing in my ears subsided upon hearing a voice. Your voice. "Breathe. Stay Calm. I'm here. Everything is going to be okay". So I did not surrender nor allow myself to scream or cry or collapse, I simply breathed. I breathed despite every leftover fragment of my being begging for me to let go. I stayed calm for the voice that asked me to. For the echo that betrayed the presence of somebody I loved.

For you.

Him

Loving him is habitual. Like my muscles always knew they would one day rest against his own. He loves me like a fool. I let him.

I describe the boy I'm in love with. How he makes me feel like white on blue and when I think of our first night together my pillow doesn't feel as cold.

She smiles.

I've gotten a hang of lying through my teeth.

The only person I've ever truly wanted was watching me write this a few minutes ago. I'm not talking about him at all. I don't care about him when it's her that's sitting beside me right now.

Resignation

There's a rumour going around that Cupid tried to quit the day we met.

The day every assigned reading in history class became nothing but another story in which we found each other. Again, and again and again.

You're a lot like that one song I love so much and insist on singing without knowing the lyrics. Because I don't know anything about this life, or what we're meant to be in it. History is doomed to repeat itself as we learned all those months ago so I suppose that explains why we keep meeting despite our yesterday's and tomorrow's. All the times we tried to talk each other into falling out of love. If I was asked to write a response to that I'd have too many points, no proof. My only proof is that I love you. And I think I always will.

Cupid packed up his bow and arrow and drafted his 2 weeks notice every time we fell apart, only to fall back together. The previous lives I loved you within no longer hold any weight. I love you in this one. You love me in this one.

Let's give him a run for his money.

I Love You More

God made me nineteen times denser than love.

Not scientifically; this conclusion was reached simply considering the fact that I've drowned in it nineteen times.

And counting.

Stardust

I'm convinced that we came from the same star. She's convinced that she didn't come from anything. She is tough and heartless, cold and loveless and while she may think all of these things to be true, the truth lies in my opposition.

While she may not see it herself, she is so beautiful. Beauty like hers cannot be breathed into something as simple as poetry and when I say she is soft and kinda and warm and heartfelt, I mean it in ways words could never begin to admit. She is generous to the point of the glass being full because her half is constantly poured into mine. Maybe there is nothing more to it. Maybe at the end of this life all of our efforts will be rendered pointless. We will be reduced back to dust and return to burning as stars in the sky, and if so, I'll be with her again.

Maybe she's wrong.

Maybe there is more. Maybe 'more' just means burning brightly together for the rest of eternity. I'm not afraid of the end in that case.

It will feel just like coming home.

Untitled 17

I Want to Save You

I'd say I'd like to be the person who saves you but I'd much rather stand beside as you did it yourself.

Many things sound better out loud than "I want to save you". So here a few subtle (maybe not so subtle) ways I'd like to help.

Let's grocery shop together. Bake cakes and flick flour, icing on both of our noses and smiles on both of our mouths.

Let's listen to our favourite albums on my bedroom floor. Explain why you felt the way you felt the first time you heard that song. You know the one I'm talking about.

Let's reminisce upon every time life proved that She loved us. Her embrace filled with photographs of people who are strangers to us now. How those moments could have lasted forever, and in a special way they did.

About the day she fell in love with somebody else and it left us spiralling on our kitchen floor. About the way we found our feet again.

Let's discuss the absurdity of this. About the universe and the sea, you before me. The questionable everything.

Let's lay in the same bed and not touch. Stare at the ceiling and explain why we ended up here in the first place.

Let's stand by the ocean and not think of anything else.

Let's not be the ones to save each other.

Let's save ourselves first.

Untitled 17

5:45 A.M.

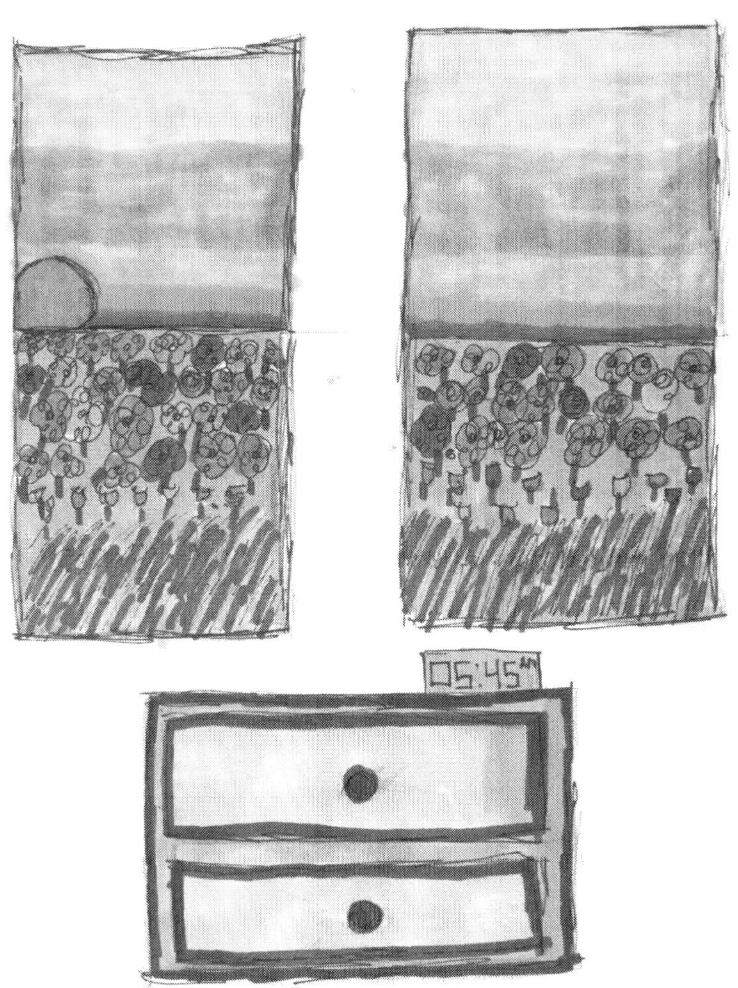

Untitled 17

fallen angel, my dear i trace shapes on your back where your wings used to be. i was sketching you against my insides while you were plucking my heart strings and reminding me of who we were and what we did and where we went. ‘they robbed you of your memories’ you murmured head tucked loosely into the crook of my neck. ‘they robbed you and you don’t remember me and my heart beats against my rib cage so loudly because i want you so badly, so completely and you don’t know who i am’. there’s this black hole in my mind where you used to live. it’s festering and stealing the best of my thoughts, everything’s tingling up my spine and I can’t help but begin to dance with your distorted heartbeats as we smile into the darkness. everything aches but its getting duller as the clock ticks and nothing hurts anymore. you didn’t know how we got here or who i was but you trusted in the divine notion that love was real and in a past life we were in love. you wanted to make it to the finish and you wanted a happy ending for us and long story short you made it far enough, then disappeared. it happened after you kissed me and i whispered to ‘go back where you belong’.

Untitled 17

all good things end in hard feelings and a whole lot of regret. i suppose i need to come to terms with that if i ever want to get over what happened. i suppose i never wanted it to happen. it to have to end. at all. i felt like a deer in the headlights when you choose me as the lucky person to receive a piece of your heart, no matter what followed. deer in the headlights because i knew that light sometimes held consequences. in my case, not quite death but close enough.

Untitled 17

italicize for emphasis, use punctuation where you see fit, bold where necessary. It's always necessary. life is amazing and everyone is happy and I want to punctuate that! look at these straight backed exclamation points. everything is an exclamation point because everything is loud and everyone is happy and everyone is dying. i would italicize dying but i don't know the oxford definition of emphasis and you told me to never use any words unless i knew what they meant. i don't know what death is and i don't know if i want to die just yet but i saw a dead bird outside a floor to ceiling window once and it reminded me of myself. i know that everything is dying and nobody is happy and that there was a bird beside it with a broken wing dragging itself to the end of the field and i think that's what people really are. there are those who are dead and there are those who break their arms trying to live. the happy ones, the ones with wings are long gone, soaring high above the others and cutting through the clouds as exclamation points because everything is amazing! the sky is so blue! so let's kiss underneath the blue because we're dying and we want to die slower than everyone else and we'll kiss and kiss and not think about the bird with the broken wing because we're flying right now and why should it concern us? look at that. i asked a question, i used a question mark and punctuated my sentence where i saw fit because i want you to love me. we're dying and we're kissing and i'll be the one to pull away first because for once in my life i want to disregard my wings and know what it feels like to be the window.

Untitled 17

i want somebody to look close enough to see everything i've been hiding. how will i know? when i fall in love again, how will i know that it wont be like last time? i'm afraid i might be destined to die alone. being shy in 2018 is like being a woman in the 60's. i can't stop picking at scabs i've created myself and i'm not sure how much of a metaphor that really is. there's a difference between heartbreak and abuse although people write about them as if they are the same. rejection is not the same as destruction. i hate how violently my hands shake. i am 17 kinds of amnesia. i am the answer to ambiguous security questions. i could die today and wait for you to forget about mourning the loss. getting better is not synonymous with going away. i am choking on my own fist in most instances. darling, live. i love you. please read this. please stay. my emotions feel like deleted voicemails. lost blood bags. is this what you wanted? i can't rhyme or write or lie the same. mommy, is this who you thought i'd become? don't answer that. i am still trying to find names for the emotions that have lied behind my eyes for decades. sometimes it is taken and never given back. i think that's just life. most nights i still miss him. missing. miss-ing. that doesn't mean i want it back. i want you to bite my lips until they bleed. i should know how to ease what has already happened, but i don't. i wish i was in love right now. i wish i was sure that was the truth. i am too distracted by the tragedies of every blue within green. i still cant sleep on his side of the bed. i want her to be able to hold me without flinching. do you remember the night you fell asleep in my passenger seat and i fell in love with your skin bathed in brake lights? me neither. my best friend called me selfish. i'm beginning to believe her. does my crumbling fascinate you? the world is too loud. i don't belong here. i am alone. i am dying. crash the car. do not resuscitate. please help me.

Untitled 17

when i say i don't care, i'm lying. congratulations. you broke my heart. i want to feel my pulse again. i want to bite down on her shoulder like warm skin is the last thing i will ever taste. learn to read between the lines. i'm in love with a girl i could never have. we are both too flirtatious with death. when you read my writing, can you see me? i suppose i'm afraid of dying with the faces of people i've hurt plastered against every lamppost on my street. missing. if i wasn't me, i think i would avoid myself at all costs. don't fall in love with me if you don't desire immortality. love either does or doesn't last forever. i'm not sure which hurts more. i'm so full of shit. these metaphors will be the death of me because sometimes i write and it feels like i'm drowning. i'm a shipwreck. if my heart beats any louder you won't be able to focus on everything i'm trying to say. wrap your knuckles in-between my vertebrae and squeeze. please break me. i need to feel something again. the ballad of a tortured artist. nothing we haven't seen before. why should it matter? do i? have i already lost? have you ever looked forward to waking up in the morning just to hear that song again? that's what being in love with her feels like. i am learning to love my hands most when they're empty. appreciate my flowers more when they wilt. treat yourself gently. it gets better with time even when you cant wake up in the morning without hitting snooze. like the night he rolled his eyes and told me to go home. i was with him, wasn't i? will anybody read this? will anybody care? do i even care? i hope nobody tries to follow me because if i had any idea where i was going i like to believe that i'd have been there by now. did you hear me? don't follow. every 18 months i give birth to new silences with names like paul and ethan and kayla and I Still Haven't Found You Yet. i can't keep pretending that i'm not tired of these teeth sitting in my lungs. some things are just impossible to say. how will i survive? the holes in my sheets are all named olivia. i want everything served to me violently, every day lived as a car crash. a punch in the chest. a blatant lie. i'll swatch your blood on my hand first to see if it complements my skin tone. i haven't let a man touch me since. i just wanted to help you love your darker parts, i never meant to become one. i am a fossil of the life once lived but has long since expired. words don't cut anymore they just ricochet and i am still so scared by loud noises. i am out of my depth here. if you love me, please tell me.

Untitled 17

YOU SAY YOU WANT TO WRITE LIKE ME BUT WHAT DOES THAT EVEN MEAN? I DON'T WRITE TO IMPRESS OR WRITE TO PRETEND, I WRITE BECAUSE IF I DON'T I MIGHT JUST EXPLODE. YOU DON'T WANT THIS. YOU DON'T WANT THIS CONSTANT ACHING, THIS CONSTANT FEAR OF NEVER BEING GOOD ENOUGH, THIS CONSTANT THIRST FOR THE THINGS THAT WILL INEVITABLY HURT YOU BECAUSE PAIN FUELS ART. YOU DON'T KNOW WHAT IT'S LIKE. YOU DON'T KNOW WHAT IT'S LIKE TO SCREAM AND CRY INTO THE STARS BECAUSE YOU FEEL SO MUCH AND CAN'T FIGURE OUT WHAT TO DO WITH IT ALL. YOU DON'T KNOW WHAT IT'S LIKE TO BE ADDICTED TO BURNING HOLES INTO YOUR SKIN BECAUSE SOMEDAYS YOUR BRAIN IS SO TIRED IT REFUSES TO FEEL ANYTHING. YOU DON'T WANT THE MIND OF SOMEBODY WHO BELIEVES SHE WILL NEVER AMOUNT TO ANYTHING. WHO'S WORDS WILL NEVER BE ENOUGH. SOMETIMES I FEEL SO ALONE IT GNAWS INTO A PIT IN MY STOMACH AND STAYS THERE UNTIL I FIND THE RIGHT SENTENCE TO SAY. MAYBE I NEVER WILL. EVERYTHING IS LOUD, THE WORLD IS SO FULL OF LIFE AND LIGHT AND NOISE BUT SOMETIMES IT ALL GETS SO OVERWHELMING I WRESTLE WITH MY GASPING HEART INSTEAD OF EXPERIENCING IT ALL. YES I SMILE. YES I LAUGH. YES I LOVE AND SING AND DANCE BUT MOST DAYS I SIT IN SILENCE TRYING TO FIND NEW METHODS TO STOP MY HANDS FROM SHAKING. I AM SO BROKEN AND LONELY AND CONFUSED, YOU COULD LOOK AT MY RIBS AND FIND THE INITIALS OF EVERY PERSON I HAVE EVER LOVED. YOU DON'T WANT TO COLLAPSE ON THE FLOOR OF A GAS STATION BECAUSE MEMORIES OF HIM SPILLING SLUSHY ACROSS THE COUNTERTOP OVERPOWER WHAT PUMP YOU WERE AT. YOU

DON'T WANT TO REMEMBER WHAT USED TO BE INSTEAD OF LEARNING HOW TO ADAPT TO WHAT IS. I JOKE ABOUT FALLING IN LOVE EVERY THREE DAYS BECAUSE ITS TRUE. I HAVE SO MUCH LOVE INSIDE OF ME, I COULD MAKE A MUSE OUT OF ANYBODY. I WAS LYING WHEN I SAID I DIDN'T LOVE YOU ANYMORE. I WAS LYING WHEN I SAID IT DIDN'T HURT. MAYBE I WILL NEVER BE WHOLE. MAYBE MY EXCRUCIATING SEARCH FOR EVERY ONE OF MY MISSING PIECES WILL BE NOTHING BUT ENTERTAINING ANECDOTES FOR MY READERS. FOR THE PEOPLE THAT "WISH THEY COULD WRITE LIKE ME" BUT DON'T KNOW WHAT IT FEELS LIKE TO BE SURROUNDED BY PEOPLE BUT STILL FEEL SO ALONE. MY FINGERTIPS HURT FROM COMING CLOSE BUT NEVER REACHING, MY PALMS ARE SCRAPED FROM HOLDING ON TO THE THINGS THAT WANTED NOTHING MORE THAN TO GET THE HELL AWAY FROM ME. I AM SO TIRED OF MY PAIN BEING TREATED DIFFERENTLY BECAUSE I AM AN ARTIST. I'M ALONE BUT I'M NOT AND IT HURTS BECAUSE ALL I WANT IS TO ADMIRE THE SKYLINE FOR WHAT IT IS AND NOT MAKE IT INTO SOME METAPHOR ABOUT WANTING TO STAY. I AM IN PAIN. I JUST USE THE RIGHT WORDS AND MAKE IT SOUND PRETTY BUT MY SKIN IS SO ITCHY. IT CRAWLS WHEN I LOOK AT THE FRIENDS WHO WILL NEVER KNOW THE TRUE EXTENT OF MY EMOTIONS. MAYBE MY BONES WILL ALWAYS CREAK, MAYBE MY CHEST WILL ALWAYS HEAVE, MAYBE MY HEART WILL ALWAYS BREAK WHEN THIS MAGNIFICENT WORLD FADES INTO NOTHING BUT BACKGROUND NOISE. MAYBE ONE DAY I WILL LOSE MY WORDS COMPLETELY AND STOP WAKING UP IN THE MORNING. MAYBE I WILL NEVER FIGURE OUT HOW TO HOLD A BEAUTIFUL THING WITHOUT BREAKING IT. MAYBE NOBODY

WILL EVER HOLD MY GAZE LONG ENOUGH TO SEE EVERYTHING I'M HIDING. MAYBE I WILL ALWAYS FIND MYSELF IN BROKEN PLATES AND ABANDONED BUILDINGS BECAUSE MOST DAYS MY EXISTENCE IS NOTHING BUT A HANDFUL OF TRIVIAL METAPHORS. MY MEMORY IS HORRIBLE BUT I CAN TELL YOU THE DETAILS OF EVERY MOMENT I'VE SPENT REALIZING EVERYBODY GROWS TIRED OF ME, EVENTUALLY. I SAY ALL THE WRONG THINGS AND MY VOICE IS TOO LOUD AND UNEVEN. I STARE AT PEOPLE MUCH LONGER THAN I NEED TO. MY STORIES ARE ONE GIANT PUNCHLINE AND SOMETIMES I'M THE ONLY ONE LAUGHING BECAUSE GOD, IT HURTS TALKING ABOUT HOOKUPS WHEN ALL I REALLY WANT TO TALK ABOUT IT TOO CONFUSING AND PRETENTIOUS TO SUM UP WITHIN UNRELENTING SMALL TALK. I JUST WANT TO BE AS BEAUTIFUL AS YOU THINK I AM. I WANT TO GIVE EVERYBODY THIS LOVE AND TICKLE THEIR SHOULDERS AND PLAY WITH THE HAIRS ON THE BACK OF THEIR NECKS AND WRITE THEM POETRY AND I WANT THEM TO STAY AND WANT ME BACK BUT I KNOW I'M NOT MEANT FOR ALL OF THAT. I'M NOT MEANT TO BE WARM AND YELLOW AND COVERED IN SUN, MY WRITING TAKES ME TOO FAR AWAY SO I SUPPOSE I WILL NEVER REALLY BE THERE. MY WRITING RESONATES BECAUSE ITS HONEST. I DON'T CHEAT YOU OUT OF ANYTHING I'VE FELT SO, TAKE IT OR LEAVE IT. I HAVE SO MUCH LEFT TO SAY BUT MY EYES HAVE GIVEN UP FOCUSING AND I HAVE GIVEN UP PUTTING IT INTO WORDS BECAUSE I'VE WRITTEN A BOOK FOR GOD'S SAKE BUT I STILL HAVEN'T FIGURED IT OUT. YOU SAY YOU WANT TO WRITE LIKE ME BUT DO YOU HAVE ANY IDEA WHAT THAT MEANS? I'M ASKING FOR MYSELF. YOUR GUESS IS AS GOOD AS MINE.

Untitled 17

shavasana in the middle of the intersection. box breathing when the walls start to close in again. the walls are closing in again. wait your turn. i would be completely alone if it weren't for your silhouette passing between the moonbeams. stop telling me that i need to do everything with more heart. i had one once and look where that got me. this room will outlive my silence. silence will outlive my long ago swallowed inability to speak. i'm not stoned, i just haven't quite finished choking down my anxiety from breakfast this morning. this all feels like trying to pull out a splinter with your fingernails. i cant forget about the way you burrowed your way underneath my skin. does anyone have a pair of tweezers i could borrow? some people stay in your heart forever, you know? it's like I'm stuck between missing you and knowing better. i do it anyways. i don't want "us" back but it would be nice to trace my fingers across the freckles on your neck one last time.

Untitled 17

everybody has so much to say about love but nothing to say when you ask why the person you love, loves somebody else. it's hard seeing the world in somebody who's trying to find their answers at the bottom of the bowl piece. she is every answer to every question and every prayer i've ever whispered but she doesn't know it. or maybe she does and she doesn't feel the same but either way it isn't her in the end. i know she's the girl of my dreams i know she's all i could've ever hoped for, all i could've ever wanted but i'm not the same to her. i know i mean something i know she loves me i really do but it hurts me so badly to see the fact that she's still hurting over somebody else. who am i without her? i love who i am now i love who i am because of her influence on my life but i'm afraid i wear my heart on my sleeve too often and i think we both know that all that ever comes from exposing your organs to the elements is pain. maybe i'm destined to perpetually ache over her and her lips and her body and her mind i think i might be falling in love with her but who knows. who says it's too late to catch myself? what happens if she's the one to catch me?

Untitled 17

i drank brandy in my coffee last night and i swore i heard your voice tucked between my bedsheets. i repeated the names of our unborn children into my notebook until i vomited because oh my god you're gone and it hurts it hurts so much i don't want to love you from afar anymore i want you back i want to suffocate in the garage with your friends one last time i want you to kiss me behind your house one last time i want your converse lying at my front door and our conversation singing through the air one last time. maybe we're not the same person after all because i feel like i'd know if you were up dry heaving at 4 am because you can never really unhear the laughter of the people who abandoned you. us coming apart felt a lot like continents forming except while i'm choking on salt water you're housing a revolution. i used to drink my coffee black and smoke a cheap cigarette just to remember the way you tasted and oh yeah i drank brandy in my coffee last night and i swore i heard your voice tucked between my bedsheets so i fell asleep on the floor.

Untitled 17

i bet you the sun gets lonely sometimes. everything revolves around him but at the same time nobody would dare touch him. is he cold inside? me too mr golden sun. i guess that's the price you pay for bathing the people you love in light. the price you pay for never dying, therefore never finding reason to lie by their side.

Untitled 17

i'm afraid of a lot of things but i think my biggest fear is being insincere. just because i've loved a lot of people before does not mean every love after that means less. i wish people could better understand that. i wish YOU better understood that. i'm in a relationship with somebody that i don't love, but i know she loves me and its terrifying. you can't force yourself to love somebody as unfortunate as that sounds. i don't love her. i'm not really sure if i love anyone. especially not myself. i want passion again. i want hot faces and fingers knotted into the hair of people i know i can't have. it inspires my art. and my heart. i suppose at the end of the day it doesn't really matter who i love because i am destined for it to never be reciprocated. somehow when it is reciprocated it ends up meaning less. i'm still trying to find the silver lining in all of this.

Untitled 17

i want to shake you by the shoulders so you know how i feel when you break eye contact. WHAT IS WRONG WITH ME? WHY DON'T YOU LOVE ME BACK? I'M TIRED OF PRETENDING TO BE CONTENT I'M TIRED OF SUPERFICIALITIES, OUR EYES ARE GLUED TO OUR PHONE SCREENS BUT MY MIND IS GLUED TO WHERE YOUR HAND IS RESTING AGAINST MY ARM. i wish you kissed me longer last night. i wish you stayed closer to me after your friends came back. i wish you came back. why didn't you ever come back?

Untitled 17

we're all so hell bent on the idea that we're trapped here. wasting away our youth and 'some of the best days of our lives'. wastes of space and time and energy. a bunch of supposedly washed out souls wondering why we feel so alone despite being surrounded by people at every corner we turn. we have to stop pretending that we aren't afraid of places unknown. of new experiences and busy streets and the harsh reality that we're all in the midst of our own disappearances. everybody is going through the same things and everybody is afraid. i'm trying my best to not be afraid. i have ambitions and i have dreams but i'm also scared that if i never venture outside of my comfort zone that is all they will ever be. i don't want that to happen. i am terrified too.

Untitled 17

thank you for letting me help in the big everything you two were creating. thank you for helping me in finding love and truth. thank you for making me feel loved and listened to and understood. i love you. i'm sorry. thank you for letting me be a part of your story. thank you for giving me the memories that remind me that i am myself. above all thank you for setting me free. thank you for loving me in my messy drunk and morning breath. in my post 10 pm sobs and daily mental breakdowns. thank you for showing me love and helping me to find acceptance in being… me. thank you for the adventures in finding myself, and who I want to be. you made me into somebody i want to be. thank you for everything. i'm not sorry anymore. but i still love you. i love you. thank you.

my time as a character in this trilogy has long since passed. things would've been easier if there was just a sequel, nothing further. i'm sorry for the shitty ending. if i had a choice i wouldn't have written an ending at all. i've always been better at writing beginnings. regardless, here goes.

it no longer matters how much it hurt. i'm just happy to see you happy. it really is over.

i guess i'm just glad it happened at all.

the end.

Untitled 17

Becoming

Untitled 17

An Ode to the Person I Will be When the Sadness Subsides

This is for the girl I will be when the depression isn't quite so heavy.

For the girl who's hands don't shake quite as violently with anxiety.

For the girl who isn't quite as sad and hopefully happy. Hopefully.

I am happy for who you are now. Trust me, I am, but don't you dare forget who you were. Who I am. You couldn't have gotten better if it weren't for me. If it weren't for my burning and trembling and bloodshed and tears. If it weren't for every projected smile that was just a little too bright to conceal everything you've spent years trying to hide. Every year you spent chasing greener grass and failing to tend to the weeds until they've outgrown everything else. You always have been quite talented at avoiding your own darkness.

I hope you've stopped mistaking your bruises for sunsets and making homes out of people who have kissed your scars and told you they were beautiful. Some things in this world are not meant to be stretched to fit within the lines of your poetry. Some words will never be enough to accurately depict what you've been through. There is nothing romantic about self-inflicted pain and in all honesty there is nothing poetic about the pain I'm in right now either. I'm honestly still struggling to find the words for all of this.

I hope you remember your mother crying when she realized she couldn't do anything to take your pain away. How violently her chest shook the day you stopped your own heart and had the darkness pumped out of you under her trembling gaze. I hope you remember the day she imagined a life lived without you and I hope you never allow another thought like that to cross her mind ever again. She acts a certain way around you because she's concerned. Not everybody can string together literary devices to depict their emotions and her showing her care for you in a different way does not mean any less than if she were to use a method by which you were familiar with. She loves you, regardless of some of the things she may say and do; you know she loves you. Hold that close to your heart forever. You are more than lucky.

I hope you remember the way your best friend spent countless hours worrying about the day you wouldn't wake up alongside the sun. Every time she drove to your house at 2 in the morning to rub your back until you fell asleep and 2 in the afternoon to bake cookies and do anything to make you smile. Most people don't have somebody who's stuck beside them through everything, but you do. The majority of lighthearted childhood stories I tell my current friends have her situated centre stage, so hold her in your heart and take the time to remind her where she stands. She is your anchor. Your compass. She helps you remain safe throughout hurricanes no matter the damage. A sisterhood through choice, not blood. That is a priceless gift. Acknowledge it once in a while.

I hope you learn to forgive yourself for your past transgressions. For every noose you've accidentally gotten tangled around other people's necks while trying to tie your own. For the boy you hurt beyond repair and every lover that ended better off without you. Forgive yourself and learn to let go. Just because your own lungs are empty, does not mean you have any right to restrict the breath of others. Your lovers should be able to exhale in your embrace and if their light dims amongst your darkness, release them gently. I promise it's only scary until your eyes adjust.

I hope you remember the first girl to walk upon scorched ground and remind you that someday it will bear fruit again. The one who bathed you in sunlight and sat beside you in comfortable silence when your loneliness became too heavy to carry alone. There is patience in loneliness and some angels can only be noticed when bathed in red brake lights. It may never come but if you get the chance to kiss her again, do nothing. Think nothing. Revel in the light of the living. The light of the woman who taught you that you've always deserved to grow towards the sun.

I hope you remember every person you've kissed to distract yourself from the aching in your chest. You couldn't care for them properly and I really do hope you've learned to deal with the consequences of that. You'll heal from every smouldering "stay" you've whispered against shoulder blades, you'll heal from every "it's not you anymore", every person who has taken your body and left your heart behind. You'll heal from perpetually missing the last train home and forgetting where home is in the first place. You'll heal, Olivia. You will.

Do you ever end up finding the right words? Does your poetry suffer once you've laid in the light again? Have sentences that don't preface longing ever tumble from your lips? Have you stopped kissing people in grave yards? Does it get easier? Do you ever end up finding what you've been looking for? What are you actually looking for?

I hope you remember the limitless love your friends showed upon every unanswerable question. Every painting and late night and hurried phone call. Every prayer stuttered through tears and gritted teeth, every cigarette put out before you reached the filter, every bad choice you made that led to the person you have become. You're a lot to handle, so much now that no metaphor can do it justice and that's saying something, coming from me. You give up often, messily and sometimes irreparably. In all honesty it's difficult to look in the mirror without feeling... hatred? Disappointment? Both?

Nevertheless, I do love you, and I want to let you know that I'm getting better every day. It is hard, but the sun always rises in the morning and I'm genuinely beginning to feel warm. The remainder of my journey won't be easy, but I know I'm finally headed in the right direction. We'll end up somewhere better. That's the only thing I'm sure of right now. The future isn't bright, but it isn't as dark anymore either. I think it is safe to say I don't quite like who I am yet, but I no longer wish to be anybody else. I think that's a good place to start.

Stay well Olivia.

I'll meet you on the other side.

Ode to Sunday Evenings

This is an ode to Sundays and every moment I've spent feeling.. everything.

Instances of hims and hers and heres and theres, goosebumps raised on inner thighs and hands grabbing, holding, touching, missing and wishing I could forget.

Sundays are supposed to be for sunsets and first kisses. Not sitting on my bedroom floor holding her shaking body in my lap as I tell her stories after the light is gone.

I read her bedtime stories, each one a different cause of her death.

The end. The end.

Monday morning and I never do end up saving anyone.

Checkmate

I am playing a game I didn't sign up for.

I am God's fantasy and for that he let me see death. I have seen death. That is to say I've seen distorted versions of myself in broken glass and side view mirrors where objects really are closer than they appear. I am closer to myself than I'd like to be.

I am nothing but a pawn in God's game against Satan.

Or maybe it's the other way around.

Bumblebee

My friends and family always tell me that I'm too hard on myself when I write. Always insisting that I was my own worst critic. Always reminding me that I have to accept writing as my way of coping. If I have to write, I should just write and not worry about the technical aspects of it. I should express my feelings without any fears of spelling or grammar. I should crush the previous belief that my writing always has to make sense to the readers.

Did I ever really write for myself?

I scoffed at them, brushed it off. Of course I wrote for myself. I was fine. Content with not being perfect. Didn't obsess over the best sounding synonym and correct use of adverbs. Why were they so concerned?

I never took what anyone said into account until the day I found a box of things from my old house on Sherwood.

I have always been convinced that I was content with my imperfections until I was attempting to decipher a multitude of scratched out and scribbled in words that sat upon the pages of an old bumblebee journal. That was when their unease didn't appear as far fetched as I had thought.

After finding that journal, I began to look though the pages of my current notebook and realized that ever since I was young, I've been editing my own diaries.

Paralysis

If I ever have another out of body experience I'll float to every moment they spent convincing me I wasn't the one anymore. I can't feel my feet anymore. I don't remember who I am some days.

Here we go again.

Me in my restlessness and need to outlive every moment spent failing to convince them that I meant something. I'm running out of patience. I am sick and I am tired and I am stopping for picnics in places I don't belong. I don't belong anywhere anymore.

If I ever have another out of body experience I hope I never come back.

I See You

This one is for the girl skipping class again.

For the girl crying in the bathroom, for the girl smoking in the parking lot, for the girl drawing hearts in the condensation on the bus window. This is for you.

I know it feels like every time you sit in the same place for too long the walls close in. I know it feels like you never were and never will be enough. I know it feels like nothing good will ever come out of living or being in a place that reeks of artificial packaging and systematic bullshit. Your mind is not meant to be kept in a box. It is not meant to be marked according to rubrics you are not meant to sit at a desk all day, writing things that don't make sense to you. Things that you don't care about. You feel alone in this. I see you and I know you do, you think you're the only person who has ever felt this way but you're not. You're an artist or a mover or a thinker. Contemplative and aching for a life that is fulfilling and teaches you more than you could ever find within an hour long power point presentation. When did you stop thinking the way you used to? When did you stop laughing? When did you stop smiling at yourself in the mirror? I know you need someone. I wonder if you feel the same things as I do, organizing and reorganizing and aligning things on your desk until you feel like you can breathe again. Talking too quietly or too loud, heart in your throat because you haven't recited your answer 46 times. 4,5,6 tiles per row on the ceiling of your first period biology class, 7,8,9 blank stares and pairs of tired eyes in your second period math class. There is more to everything than you think. I see what is simmering beneath the surface and it is a potential you could never even imagine.

Maybe you won't succeed in school. Maybe you won't make honour roll. Maybe you'll fail chemistry with an 11% when science used to be your passion. Maybe you won't graduate with all of your friends and in the grand scheme of things maybe you'll realize that none of that really matters. You will arrive at your destination eventually. Everybody gets there differently and if you get there by taking time away from your suffocating class rooms every once in a while so be it. Fuck all the people "congratulating" you for coming to class, kick them in the head for all I care just remember that friends are not always going to act like friends. You're doing your best, I can see it. I can see the heart you drew in the condensation. It's an artistic interpretation of the diagram from biology class. I wish I had the guts to tell you I think that it's pretty.

I know you need someone.

Let me be your someone.

Peachy Keen Jelly Bean

I fill my emptiness up with anything else because it makes it much easier to lie about. Why do I drink so much peach vodka? Why am I always falling in love? My life is so funny and ironic the way I phrase it. Telling stories where I slit my own wrists in the end. Everybody laughs when they hear how silly I am. How often I fuck up. Sometimes it gets to the point where nobody trusts me to do simple things because I'm just "too wild". How am I? I'm peachy. I never do my homework. Am quick with jokes, but not to laugh. Every one of my punchlines is just another tragedy. Of course I'm having a great time… Of course I'm having a great time! Give me another shot of vodka. I'm peachy. The last time I felt anything? I can't remember, but it doesn't matter because there's always another story to tell. Another extra box of cupcakes and another ex and another fuck up and another joke and everything is just peachy.

Impurities

Picking at your scabs and trying to turn it into poetry never works out the way you want it to. Maybe you enjoy the sting. Maybe you enjoy the reassurance that wounds can heal, although that doesn't account for the fingerprints on your neck that never seem to fade. There is a certain chaos in longing for the things that have hurt you the most. Your name still burns my tongue. I never learned to cool you off before inviting you inside, I swear you could be a ghost. If ghosts were warm and kind and… human. I pick at the scabs myself yet still find ways to blame all of the bloodshed on you. Your flame provides such contrast against the frigidness I used to believe the world to be bathed in and you melted me. Burned me. Made my scabs itch so intolerably that I had to pick them. You leave me too raw. Too vulnerable.

I still can't seem to find the poetry in that.

Dark Rooms

Who are you when the room goes dark? When the mask is peeled off at the end of the day? Who are you when the credits roll? When the interlude plays? Why are you so afraid to be who you are? Your words will move mountains, your touch could start revolutions yet you are sitting in the corner muting yourself for the sake of being loved by the world. Love the world but please, pay no regard to how much it loves you because when the lights go out we are all the same. Blood and bones and lungs and hearts, eventually beating together in tandem. Be yourself. Be beautiful. Be the person you are when the lights go out. Furthermore, continue to be that person when the sun rises again in the morning. Do not mute who you are, for hearts will always beat alongside yours and love every piece of you for the sole fact that you are alive. For the sole fact that you, are you.

In the dark we are all the same, so ask yourself this.

Who are you? Really?

Happy Thoughts

Why would you wish for me to write about happier things when you've witnessed the darkness I hold so dearly to my chest? A lot of my poetry is sad because I am sad. It's actually quite simple.

If you want a happy poem you'll need to skip a few chapters.

Go on. I don't blame you. My fairy Godmother gave me the terrible gift of having words trapped in my lungs and I suppose that explains why I'm always breathing like there's something caught in my throat. I say I am in love with death. With girls and the ocean, I kiss exhaust pipes and closed garage doors and CO2 and veins unfolded to the sky. How could you see all of these things and still say nothing? Maybe I thought that if I let other people watch me fall apart they would care enough to put me back together themselves. Maybe all of my poetry is nothing but a study of human emotion… or lack thereof. My love affairs with speeding trains and bottles of Benzos are far from over so maybe that means I'm close to failing. Have I already failed? Failure, triumph, does it really matter if everything is already over? I am insane, narcissistic, psychotic and abusive. I'm a bitch and an attention whore. I'm insensitive, self-indulgent, disingenuous.

"Olivia this poem is too sad".

If you want a happy poem you'll need to skip a few chapters.

Villainous

We always seem to paint evil as very bad or very ugly.

The dark forest is evil and the lush treetops are pure.

Evil is never ordinary.

Evil is never dark brown hair and a kind smile.

Evil is never the person staring back at you in the mirror.

Until you're hurting everybody you love.

Until you're spitting venom and not caring for the consequences.

Until it is.

Tomorrow

The alarm blares. I hit snooze. Maybe tomorrow.

Control is a notion I've rarely felt familiar with in any setting other than dreams. It never snows here. All of the trees are old, strong, alive, whispering secrets to me when I can't sleep. I venture into gas stations to find love and they never ID. Too young to know better, too old to care, balancing on the precipice between childhood and whatever else is out there. Some nights I find myself floating to his doorstep and I can't control him screaming "LEAVE. THIS ISN'T REAL. GO HOME". My mouth glues shut. I still can't admit that I don't know where home is anymore. Some nights I wake up tangled in her arms and I would honestly do anything to say it one last time. You saved me. The sun doesn't set until I'm ready. The audio recordings explaining the way the world came to be are finally rewound and I find the grace within mistake. Unhinge, unlock, close, deadbolt. Every bridge leading me back to the people who hurt me erupt into flames. Some nights I am alone here. Left to stare at my misshapen features in the mirror. Each instance a reflected variation of the truth. I'm beginning to find peace in that. Maybe I am cut out for reality. Maybe I'll make it out okay. Maybe there's beauty in the amount of times I've promised myself tomorrow. I wonder what worlds await me on the other side.

The alarm blares. I hit snooze. Maybe tomorrow.

Untitled 17

The Things We Don't Talk About

We don't talk about the flyers on the front porch that we were too lazy to bring in after school. We don't talk about the neighbours at the end of the street. We don't talk about the fact that his name is still in my mouth when I'm in love with you. We don't talk about how it feels to fall out of love with each other. We don't talk about the possibility that we are not right for each other. We don't talk about the inevitability of separating after high school. We don't talk about when you asked your grandmother for a bowl of soup and she brought you coffee. We don't talk about my fathers cancer. We don't talk about last May. We don't talk about what it felt like when my heart stopped beating. We don't talk about the way my mother cried. We don't talk about the monsters living inside my chest. We don't talk about the fact that he loved me so much he invited them to stay in his own and we definitely don't talk about how despite how hard he tries, due to everything, he will never be able to love me again. We don't talk about the big oak tree in the backyard of my childhood home being the safe zone for tag. We don't talk about being so scared to play we stayed "safe" for the majority of the game. We don't talk about how if I had the chance to go back there I would press myself against the tree until I felt safe again.

We don't talk about how I'm not safe anymore.

Let's keep it that way please.

Orange Peel

Instead of gradually peeling back your layers to arrive at the centre, some bite right into you.

They will think you to be something less than sweet but pay mind to the fact that this is no fault of yours.

They are tasting the rind.

It's okay to be bitter.

In-between Being

I am a being of in-betweens. Almost's. Maybe's. Could've, should've … didn't. My existence consists of "they could have loved me … but they didn't". It consists of those words clumped into a ball at the back of my throat because I can't come to terms with that. I am a receiver of empty words. Somebody who sees the world in others and while promises of reciprocation come, they are never quite delivered. Do I really radiate goodness or do people just say that because it feels like the right thing to do? I am caught between artistry and reality. If I continue to view the world through rose tinted lenses I will never truly live. Everybody has their own agenda. Everybody loves to love. I was almost worthy of love. I should've learned to love myself a long time ago, but the line between self love and self obsession has blurred. I refuse to reach a day where I lack self awareness. I am somewhere in-between pessimism and optimism. I am somewhere in-between concrete and abstract. I am somewhere in-between happy and miserable. My existence sits somewhere in-between Olivia and Grace. I will never conform to anything therefore I will never be enough.

I am somewhere in-between not being and being okay with that.

Mosaic

They say that once I've healed I will finally feel whole again.

How do I tell them the only way I know how to live is in fragments?

I push at the bruises and peel away the scabs because I want to feel something.

How are they supposed to know I constantly sabotage my own healing?

They want to see me get better.

How are they supposed to know that I don't know how?

No Hard Feelings

Whenever somebody asks to move on I can't help but flinch.

More often than not they will ask to bury the hatchet without clarifying that my back is the site of the funeral.

Empty Notebooks and Espresso

"Can you see the moon from where you are?"

I'm back to drinking black coffee and bleeding into a notebook that doesn't care about the weight of my words. I am sad again. People are always leaving they all come and they go go go I share my heart with them and they throw it away and I'm tired of it. I'm tired of everything I want to be more than a bruise more than a moment of speechlessness more than a memory more than a disappointment more than a "but she had so much potential". I'm cutting away at the hurt and whats left looks like an abandoned building. It feels appropriate. I am a burnt out star, a should have been could have been would have been. A dried out corn husk, a rotten fruit rind, an untouched notebook… this is me. This is who I've become.

I am empty.

I have nothing left.

"No. All I can see is burnt out stars"

Untitled 17

The Beauty of Being

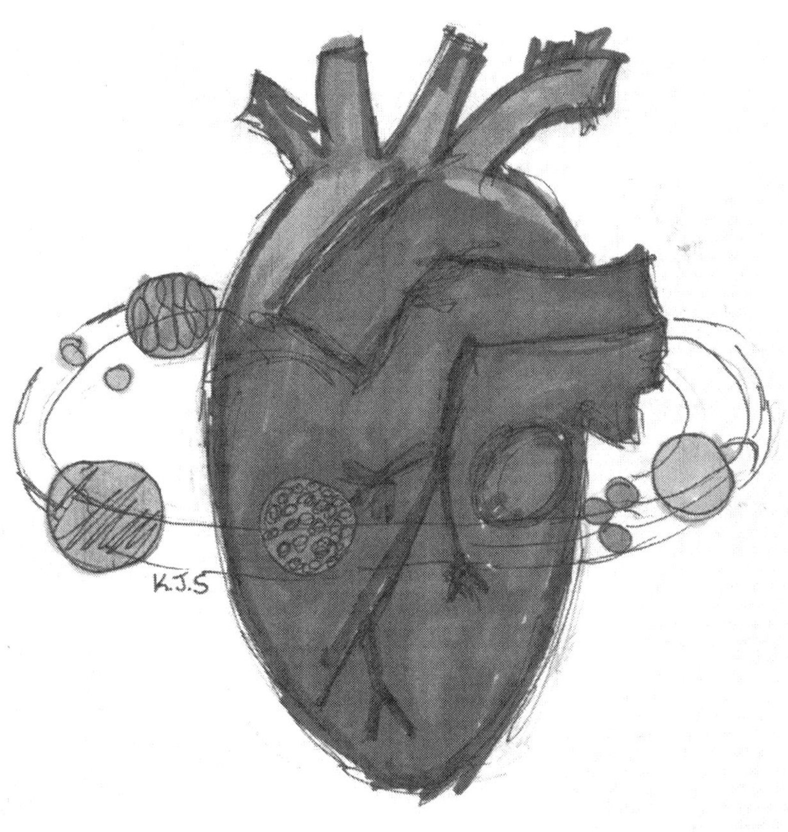

Remedial

There are seemingly insignificant moments that I know I am always going to remember.

Moments when a good song is playing in the background and you're with people who love you . The music thumps in your chest and nobody is on their phone because the moment is too rich to be accurately captured within a 10 second snapchat.

Today I laughed so hard I could barely breathe and realized how much I love certain aspects of living. It was warm outside. The sun is setting and my room is a pretty shade of pinkish purple. I feel elated. Lungs filled, heart beating. My bed is made with polaroid pictures I never found the heart to throw away because I am always going to love the faces within them. Screw hard feelings, I'm beginning to accept that that's okay. I'm beginning to savour the noise as deeply as I savour the quiet, allowing every night like this to linger in every right way. I am falling back into love with my life and suddenly everything feels just the slightest bit more right again. I am young and I am healthy and the coming days are so good.

I am here and I am happy and I am alive.

I feel alive again.

The Search Continues

I know how badly you want to die and how deeply you believe that life is meaningless and we will all eventually return to dust but have you ever looked at the sky? Like, really looked at it? Have you ever stared into a pair of brown eyes while they're being hit by sunlight and they turn that yellowy, caramel colour like the time you put too much creamer in your coffee? Have you ever watched your best friend rap the verse of a song perfectly and throw her head back in laughter after you had never believed you could be happy again? Have you ever finished a good book and had to curl up in tears because you had never felt more understood? Have you ever felt that understood by another human being? Have you ever felt that tug in your heart strings while with someone that urges you to say a silent prayer to the universe? Like you were once so in love you didn't believe it needed to be stated out loud? Have you ever woken up in the morning and felt thankful for it? Thankful for another sunrise? Another sunset? Another chance to be different? Better? Have you ever learned to let go of the past? Of what's hurt you? Of who didn't care? Have you ever found the peace in that?

These feelings will come one day. You will thank yourself for staying alive. Love is coming, and it will come once you stop searching.

Stop looking for the answers and they will find you.

Small Victories

Today I said I wanted to kill myself out of habit.

This was only significant because it was the first time I've ever said it without meaning it.

Warranted Tears

Sometimes there is nothing left to do but to cry. Cry for the people you love. Cry for the people you've lost. Cry for who you were, who you are, who you're going to be. Cry for the sunrise and cry for the sunset. Cry for nature and cities and strangers and family and cats and coffee and old books and everything. Cry for the beauty of everything.

You are a part of this magnificent everything.

Crying proves we're still alive.

Whole

Its hard to deal with the hollowness when it splits you wide open and forces you to tape back together the pieces in the morning. It's hard to realize you forget who you are, who you were and feel indifference towards who you're becoming. It's hard to fight and cry and claw at the cliff's edge. Its hard to hold on for dear life but maybe its worth it. Sometimes it feels so beautiful to wake up in the morning. Humid air filling my lungs feels so warm, and right. Maybe its worth it because warmth and sunlight make everything feel okay again. I'm alive, and I'm beginning to think that that's all that really matters. Despite being damaged and knowing that nobody can fix me, the sky looks so pretty at night. The feeling you get when you dance with your best friends, wine drunk at 3 in the morning. The way the sunrise hits their eyes and makes you believe in something so much bigger than yourself. Life continues, it always does and moving on from others makes me so unbelievably sad but the way sand feels in between your toes never changes. Your memories will always be your memories. There to comfort you when everything feels too lonely to bear. My memories have gotten me through more than the people within them will ever know. These past 17 years have been anything but easy, yet the way the people in my life make me feel proves that I am meant to be here. What I have been through dictates what I have conquered. My life is now so full of light and calm and happiness so I know its worth it. For them, I know its worth it to keep going, even when it hurts. It's all for them.

For you.

Content

I'd really like to write an ode to these moments however I fear that if I do they will no longer be mine. I'm content to share them with people so long as it remains within a select few. The right few. There's something about the sun setting over the city you grew up in. The city you spent years aching and stumbling and wasting time in with the people who stayed after the sun sank below the skyline. Do you think of anybody when you watch the sun set? People who are personifications of the phrase "the sun always rises again in the morning". It always does. They always do. What's their name? They spend their days bathing my favourite moments in shades of orange that could make the sky I am writing this beneath sick. Euphoria, nirvana, salubriousness, contentment, every abstract adjective I would never use to describe this moment. Memories like these don't warrant description. I wonder if they'll ever know how many times I've chosen to exhale simply because they are willing participants within my moments. Content. I am not quite happy yet, but I'm getting there. Stay close to the people who give you sunrises after the sun sets. It's not much. But it's enough for me.

Fifteen Things

Let this stand as a tribute to the coping mechanism that has carried me thus far. Fly to wherever your heart desires most. When you feel as if you don't belong anywhere know that within me and my poetry, you belong everywhere. Most days I try to pretend that this world is treating you better than it has treated me. You may not be able to see the bravery, beauty or resilience in yourself because it's perceived as just survival. Because sometimes its just another day of trying to make it to school; or get out of bed. Every moment you are all fighting a war I can't see but despite that; remember that in the face of every battle you will always have me on your side.

Right there behind you. Where will you fly?

1. The bus stop where they came and they went and you stayed standing there.

2. The trampoline I laid on in 6th grade, staring at the stars with my two best friends. Unknowing of how soon those innocent moments would be over.

3. The place where I left bruises on somebodies heart because I didn't know how to properly treat my own. Helped him pack his bags to move on to a place of understanding and genuine love. A place where the paper never cuts.

4. My grandmother's attic where my cousins and I sat our first Christmas without grandpa, revelling in the knowledge that nothing would ever be the same as before.

5. Devil's punchbowl to watch all of the lights come on at night. To grab her hand one last time and admit that it will always be her.

Untitled 17

6. The bakery where I serve cupcakes and allow the ovens to warm my back. I scrub dishes happily with nowhere else to go and no one else to be.

7. Every younger version of myself, where we were all innocent and full of life, not knowing all of what was to come. Everything we did not and could not know. Every world awaiting us.

8. The leather chair in his basement where we sat tangled in each other last winter to look him in the eyes and say it one last time. I love you.

9. Every night I drove with no direction. Laughing or crying hysterically, feeling the true intensity of emotion regardless.

10. The cottage in Muskoka where I fell in love with my art. Where I fell in love with my best friend.

11. My father's hospital room where I danced behind curtains. Not knowing if the cancer was gone for certain but revelling in the fact that he was alive. We were alive.

12. The moment where I knew. Where the VHS tapes of the ones that got away could not be rewound and where I recognize the grace within regret.

13. The moment I knew I could not go back, regardless of my wings. I cannot fly anywhere that explains why everything happened the way it did, nor explain what's to come.

14. The moment where we finally know all of these things and I still chose to be right here, in the living, anyways.

15. The living.

Untitled 17

If you're anything like me and you believe in signs from the universe, this is it.

Simple Moments

Take the time to remember what it is that's keeping you here. Whether it be a who, a how or a where. Along the way you will meet people who make everything feel like your heart is breaking in reverse. You will drown in love and life and deciding to stay a million times over. Gratitude towards sticking around long enough to see beautiful things. To seeing at all. Sometimes the sky is so blue it reflects my smile in sunlight as if to say "Hello. I don't know who you are, but I know I've been waiting for you".

The Light Behind Your Eyes

You've always had light behind your eyes regardless of who you were looking at; if anybody at all.

It has always been there.

Always will be.

You were the one who put it there.

Remember that when they try to come for your warmth and saturation. Remember that when "they" turn into yourself.

Remember that.

Everything More

In case I ever lose this memory once everything is said and done and dead please remember this. Remember how through your tears they slow danced with you to Frank Sinatra and helped you pull down the ceiling with nothing but their fingertips. Romantic love is no longer a muse. I think this is a sign from God or whatever else is out there that romantic love isn't meant to be a controlling factor within my life right now. You can't always get what you want and I think there's beauty in that eventually. I feel freer. Less sad somehow. I think the worst part is that everyone is fascinated by me yet nothing past curious. But I know they are different. They care enough to get so much closer. To do everything more than observe.

Untitled 17

Oceans

I put the conch shell to my ear and suddenly I knew more about living than I did about dying.

I knew more about love than loss and I could look my faults in the face without flinching. Suicide notes have been rewritten into postcards because dear god am I happy to be here. And I don't wish it to be any other way. "I wish you were here". While I may not be, you are. That's the only thing that really matters.

Don't you get it? Don't you understand you're meant to sleep soundest in your own arms?

I watched myself grow, slowly but surely. Tending to the gardens gently and to my heart gentler. My arms empty from the people I couldn't love before and I finally find the magnificence in loneliness.

When I find the magnificence in hearing the ocean when my ears are plugged by my own two hands.

Untitled 17

Lighthouses

Untitled 17

I would be a lost cause without you. Please know I am thankful for everything and that I love you. Infinitely. Thank you all for being there to guide me through the dark.

Yours Truly,
Liv Grace

P.S. If any of these tributes correlate to the way you feel about somebody in *your* life, send it to them.

My words are just as much for your somebodies as they are for mine.

Untitled 17

To : The Girl Who Always Will Be Home

You are my best friend. My sister. My soul mate. The girl who always will be home. My first and likely last love all wrapped up into one. When I see my future I see us sitting at the dinner table with our respective families. Us laughing over the memories only we share. I like that idea a whole lot. I don't need much as long as I have you. And I know I have you. You been there for me through absolutely everything. From getting food poisoning, to crying over boys and girls, to holding my hand during the toughest few days of my life. Every hilarious, ridiculous memory has been my solitude whenever the world becomes too much to bear. You were and always will be my rock.

I remember the night we sat in my step-brother's car, tossing a mango back and forth, screaming Florence and the Machine at the top of our lungs. You looked so crazy and free and beautiful. The sky was tinted an orangey-purple and for the first time in a long time I remember feeling lucky to be alive. You have been there through the brightness and the darkness and every shade of light that growing up together has brought upon us. Life is hard, but the way you make me laugh reminds me of the future. It reminds me of how badly I want you to be in it, as well as the underlying positivity that you're not going anywhere. Ever. We may grow up and inevitably grow apart but God, I am so lucky to have been able to call you my best friend. Somebody who never really "partied" or drank or smoked because being around her solidifies the belief that you don't need drugs or alcohol to feel invincible.

Have you ever met somebody who knows you're upset before you do? Who knows your mind and your mannerisms like the back of her hand? Who supports you through everything and makes you laugh at all of the horrible parts of life? Makes you forget about what you're upset about in the first place? When we were three years old I reached for your hand in ballet class and you pulled away. When we were 15 years old you reached for my hand when I couldn't hold on to anything at all. You held on when I pulled away. To this day you have never let go. I hope you know how much that means to me. You have given me so many adventures in the past few years whether it be driving around for hours, teaching you about genetics over pancakes, or simply sitting at home, making odd sounds and laughing until our lungs collapsed. That's what a best friend is after all. Somebody who makes everything feel exciting. You are my Saturday night party and my Sunday morning breakfast in bed. You are quiet bookstores and purring cats, somebody who I've always known I've needed and always known I've had. You're my other half. My other three quarters I should say. You cut me slack when my own selfish needs get in the way of you living the life you deserve. Nothing is ever picture perfect but your existence reminds me that sometimes life isn't meant to be so. You recognize the tide and know when to fight. You fight regardless of whether or not it is your battle. We may live within an unfinished world but somehow you have the ability to make me feel whole, granted I am one of the most broken people I have ever met. I hope one day you create your own definition of being whole too. I've never met somebody who has put themselves before others without hesitation or request for compensation as frequently as you do. While you may never admit it, you emanate love. My goal is to embody the love and light you have taught me to see simply by… being. I love you without end. You are off to bigger, better and brighter things. These things entailing time spent apart. We grew up together but I know it's about time we learned how to grow on our own. I want you to know that it isn't your obligation to jog in place forever. It's okay to take a break every once in a while. Wherever the world takes us, I want you to always know that she has somewhere to call home, in me. I want to thank you for teaching me the beauty that comes with loving somebody so much you would do anything for them. I want it to be known that I'd do absolutely anything for you. Have you ever found your home within a person? I have.

Girl who always will be home, words will never do you justice. You are too great of a human being to ever hope to be summed up in a paragraph on a piece of paper. You're simply everything to me. Absolutely fucking everything. Life will go on, but every once in a while I hope you remember to come home to me. Wherever you may go, I want you to remember us and the everlasting impact you had on my heart, my soul, my mind, every essence of my being. I wouldn't be me, without you. To the girl who always will be home, I love you. Without end.

P.S. Whenever you're reading this, I'll come home soon. I pinky promise. Even though that's not our thing.

To : The Brother I Never Knew I Needed

You know that I grew up as an only child and I suppose I've always envied you for your family because before you came around I never entertained the thought that I was lonely. But I was. I don't know who I'd be today if I had grown up with siblings, but I do remember drowning in my loneliness after fights with my mom because I simply had no one else. Our friendship didn't start like most. At first you were just some boy whose father happened to marry my mother and now lived in the same house as me. I'm not sure if you remember but we butt heads a lot when we were younger. It's funny to think about now because from tenth grade onwards you became my best friend. Through every Friday night abandoned building adventure, late night drive, evening spent listening to me cry at the brow, and simply growing up together, I never knew I could have wanted a brother. Then you came along.

It's a little sad that we're never going to have that again. That youth. That blatant irresponsibility and freedom. Thank you for experiencing it all with me though. We were pretty damn lucky if you think about it. Windows down, Gambino blaring, food everywhere, driving with no destination (you seriously wasted so much gas money on me). Through every rant and drive home from the dangerous shit I used to get myself into I knew I now had someone incredibly special in my life

We may not be blood related but I am positive that you're the best brother in the world. You also happen to be one of the best things to ever happen to me. So thank you. Not only for existing but for caring about me as if we were blood related. It means the world. I don't think I've ever said this out loud but you're my role model. I not only look up to you as a brother, but as a person I want to be like when I'm older. I'm so proud of you and the life you are creating for yourself, despite the hard times. Here's to the art you will create, new songs you'll discover, things you will learn, people you'll meet, world's you'll change. Here's to your future. I don't think you have any idea how bright that is. I don't think you understand how hard I cried the day you left for university. It felt like I was losing a piece of myself. But I know you're happier now (at least trying your best to be) and working towards making this world your own. And it is. You are more capable than you give yourself credit for and I hope one day you'll come to know that.

I love you. I never say that enough, but I do.

Thank you for being the brother I never knew I needed. Thank you for being a constant reminder that no matter how lonely I was growing up, I have you now.

Untitled 17

To : The Girl Who Carried Me Through the Dog Days

I never ended up buying that orange lighter you suggested all those months ago. Maybe we can go pick one up some day soon. Scream that the dog days are over despite how frequently our voices crack. Because we're still in the midst of them. The dog days are still here and prevalent as ever before but, we're here too. You're here too. I'm beginning to believe that that's all that really matters. Who else would listen to my shaky voice reciting poetry every night I want to cry, but don't? Who else would grab my hand in the darkness on the nights when I do? If we had visited the naive, broken people we were a year ago I doubt they would have seen this coming. You're my best friend, you know? You picked me up on the days I couldn't stand tall. You carried me through some of the worst dog days and pushed me forwards when I couldn't do it myself. You were also there for the ones we found ourselves smiling within, in spite of everything. Peering over the other side of the bridge in the forest. Reclaiming every song that used to make us bleed. Dancing carelessly around my bedroom, cleopatra on repeat until we fell asleep. I still listen to that playlist you made me sometimes. When I say I love you I mean that I think I was waiting for you my whole life. When we met you couldn't give me what I wanted, but over the past year you've managed to give me exactly what I need. Which is you. Everything about you. I hope you know how effortlessly beautiful you are. How effortless it is for me to love you even on the the days you curl every sharp thing you can find close to your chest. When I write letters to the moon I tell her about that. About you. How you became the absolute world to me. About the love I had for you until I realized we were not meant to love each other like that. You loved me differently than I loved you but you still loved me. Thank you for loving me. We still have many battles left to fight but if this world has taught us anything it's that we're capable of winning together. I can't wait to win with you by my side.

The dog days are far from over but I know you'll be beside me until they are. With your obnoxious laugh and Fruitopia stained t shirts. Our aimless drives and childish adventures. Everything we've experienced together that convinced us that maybe life wasn't so bad after all. My life isn't so unbearable, thanks to you. Despite the innumerable bad times I think at the end of everything, I'll look back on the dog days with a knowing smile. I'm afraid I may love you until the day that I die. Everything I am now is thanks to you.

Once the dog days are finally over, I think they'll be my favourite part.

To : The Boy With The Forest in His Eyes

This is a tribute to what we could have been if we had met at a different time. A tribute to all of the maybes that could have been memories. Maybe in another lifetime we built that house on the beach with the huge windows in the living room. The lifetime where we lived in the studio apartment with all of the potted plants hanging from the ceiling, paint on both of our faces for no reason other than being together made us want to create. Maybe you still feel my warmth when you hear my laugh in public and think of all the lifetimes we spent laughing together. Growing old together. All of the lifetimes you took me to see Monet's work in person but I was too busy staring at you. Maybe in another lifetime you asked me to stay instead of screaming "just leave, I'm too fucked up", although I do know that those two exclamations are sometimes synonymous. Maybe in another lifetime you came back to me and I kissed your collarbone and told you that everything would be okay. Maybe in another lifetime we're okay. Maybe in another lifetime we'll do what we really want and that will end with both of us in the same bed with the lights dimmed, not off, nostalgia ultra playing in the background from an unidentifiable source. Maybe in another lifetime you won't stop loving me. Or realize that even when you said you stopped, you didn't. You are so beautiful, and confused, and enigmatic. It is neither my fault nor yours that we met at the wrong time in this lifetime. Although I wish to see you happy someday, it burns to meet the realization that your happiness will no longer connote my presence.

Just know in the lifetime where all of this worked out and no bloodshed ever took place between us, I'm laying in our bed right now, staring at the stars, waiting for you. In the lifetime where the alarm clock never went off.

To the boy with the forest in his eyes, I left the lights on. Come home soon.

Untitled 17

To : The Girl With The Triangle Tattoo

This one is for the girl who took me to the only rooftop I've ever visited and not wanted to jump off of. For the girl who dances to Hey Ya every time it comes on like there's no such thing as shame. She is everything I wanted to be when I was younger. My heart stays aching in my chest when I tell her things and she gets it. Because I know she gets it. And I wish she didn't. No one can say she isn't beautiful because she is, she is, she *is*, she has taken the darkness by the skin of its teeth and thrown it away, so far away that I hope she never again forgets what it feels like to lay in the light of the sun. She has seen death. Time and time again she struggles to face her own mortality and I know that she's thought there would never come a day when she would stop crying but there has. I wonder if she knows why I cried so hard the last time I saw her. I wonder if she knows she has finally become the embodiment of a life that no longer aches to end. I truly do wonder if she knows how inspiring that has been for me to hold on to. When I say her name it feels like waterfalls. Flooding every molecule of my brain with her because she is. And she always will be. The fear of god in the presence of naked sinners, she is the dance the sky performs after a lightning storm. Purple veins exploding on eyelids, Doc Martens tapping (always fucking tapping) upon wooden floors performing that adorable little dance she does when she's nervous. A woman blossoming in on herself into something that makes me question if I ever truly knew what beauty was in the first place. And I know there are pieces of her that still taste like last year. All the bitter and hardened roots but still she blooms because recognizing blood stains for what they are is much better than pouring bleach into open wounds. Maybe this is pretentious, maybe it doesn't make sense but I think the whole point of this is to tell her that she makes me feel alive. For now light triumphs dark and they've always told her that that's a good thing and I'm beginning to believe that they meant it.

I hope she does too.

To : The Passionately Broken Record Boy

I am becoming whole with a cause and he made me believe that there was a reason for everything. I met him in this life, two weeks after I couldn't fasten the rope in my basement, two desks to the left, one back. Quiet boy with soft smile, head down, leg tapping. Picture me one desk up, two desks to the right unknowingly sitting metres away from the truest human being I would experience thus far. The human being who would introduce me to new genres of music, run through sprinklers with me, sit talking for hours smoking full packs of cigarettes, walk through forests, introduce me to genuinely hilarious people and help me experience the true beauty of not being okay. The human being jealous of music and the broken people that made it. The boy like his father; or so he tells me every time he's drunk. Stop looking in the mirror trying to find darkness where there is none. Light another cigarette, we're all going to die someday. Drown in your own self hatred, the water's warmer in the deep end and I'll help you keep your head above the water if you promise to float beside me when the sun rises again.

Once he said he'd kill himself in every universe he experiences without me and maybe so but even with me in his universe I wonder if he means it when he agrees that we should stay. I hope he stays. Sweaty-palmed handshakes, aching and aching he is as soft as the skin beside his eyes when he smiles. Why try to act so sharp edged when your heart is made from all things gentle? Passionately broken record boy, repeating the same things over and over again under the influence with undertones of love for others. The love he's unable to show towards himself. I see the way his shoulders curve downwards on the worst days, trying to make himself smaller to fit inside some new definition of "lovable". The only person to ever tell me i was easy to love and prove it. I don't know if I've ever thanked him for that. Passionately broken record boy, appreciating my art and leaving me to wonder if the words we've shared after midnight had the same effect on his heartbeats as they have had on mine. Sometimes he looks at me innocently but not so innocently because I'm sure he's held my gaze at least once long enough to see everything I've been hiding. I'm never really sure if he's joking or not. About life and love and wanting to die. I want to tell him that I love him in the way I love every person I've ever lost. Like I sleep with my shoes on in case there comes a night I have to chase after him. He is the sum of everyone he has ever loved minus the drug addictions and prostitutes and self-inflicted stab wounds. It scares me that despite cold skin his presence keeps me warm and I am warm, I am warm, I am warm. I have never felt so warm and secure and void of anxiety within a pair of arms before and maybe him entering my life as carelessly and beautifully as he did was one of the reasons for everything. I genuinely believe it was.

Passionately broken record boy. I didn't meet him in the past life, two weeks after I fastened the rope in my basement, two desks to the left, one back. Quiet boy with soft smile, head down, leg tapping. Picture an empty chair. One desk up, two desks to the right, never having the chance to know the truest human being I would've experienced thus far. An empty space of a person he knew of but never knew.

But in this life I did have the chance. I got to know *him*, not just a tragic biography. Not just a tragic suicide told enthusiastically by those who ached to follow. I knew him. I know him. Five months after I couldn't fasten the rope in my basement we were staring into the stars in comfortable silence and I finally believed that there was a reason for everything.

I am becoming whole with a cause.

And the cause is him.

Untitled 17

To : The Girl With The Aura of Orange

I asked her today what some of her favourite things about this world were and she answered.

She said she loves sunsets and forests and mountains and old cities you can feel the history of. Frank Sinatra on vinyl, long car rides with no destination, the colour orange and learning. Always learning. I see her in every single one of these things. The things that make her heart ache much like the nameless orange hue that bathes the sky at dusk, when most people haven't gone outside to appreciate it yet (but the ones who do never forget that moment). Just because nobody captures a magnificent turning of the sun on their snapchat story does not mean that it didn't occur, it just means some things need to be experienced and not discussed. She's a lot like that. I hope she falls in love a little later on for that exact reason. Nobody at this age will be able to do her justice and maybe she's always felt a little out of place because she's spent so many years attempting to reduce herself to small places. Like a butterfly afraid of leaving its cocoon because being a caterpillar was all it had ever known before. Her wings are gorgeous, all things considered. She should never abridge her being to fit this superficial idea of romantic love because one day somebody will want her, all of her, so much of her all at once because there is so fucking much to love. She is it. She is everything and I will dedicate my nights of stillness to reminding her that. When I'm silent I hope she hears me saying "I hope you're doing okay. I hope people stop disappointing you. I hope everybody who witnesses your smile knows how lucky they are. I hope your bed embraces your shoulders every night, appreciating the constellations of freckles that render the stars envious." She still fits so perfectly in small places but there's something magical about how she's taken life by the throat and whispered "you're mine", even when her voice shakes. There's something magical about the flowers growing at the bottom of a mountain in Victoria that directly correlated with how I feel about her existence. Something that remains, growing and spreading colour despite being cold.

Untitled 17

She is ever changing and despite fearing "never being good enough" this coming of age narrative has got it all wrong. As long as she is changing she will never be "good enough". Good enough connotes a point of reference. There are no reference points now because she is alive and I'd still be heartbroken if I were to ever learn she doesn't view that as a miracle in itself. She is every wrong turn I have ever taken that has led me to a beautiful place. She is the trail of flower petals that help me find my way back home. She is finding new ways to breathe and that breath sometimes fills my own lungs because how does somebody exist in that much beauty and remain unaware of it? She is Frank Sinatra on vinyl. I see her in music and the people who have been good to her because if you have ever meant something to her she would never allow you to forget. She still unravels when the sky is gray but this time I know she will make it out alive without receiving bouquets of outstretched hands. Most hands cross fingers behind their backs anyways and genuine promises have always been better suited to her. Waking up waist deep in the sorrow of your former selves is difficult however she rises above. Rises, rises, always rising, history never does repeat itself and the rain never apologizes for falling and she should never apologize for her laughter. The kind that bubbles from within her chest and forces her cheeks apart until they turn numb. Happy is different, and different is good. All I've ever wanted was to hear that somedays she laughs so hard her stomach clenches. Dear god I've missed that. She is interlocked fingers and french toast, the summer we met and never stopped saying "I love you", the speech on something she full heartedly believes in.

Everything remains interconnected. Her, her ancestors, my ancestors. I swear she was my sister in another life. I find solace in the things that hold on to you even after you've quit. Rest assured if that thing is a person with their own experience in letting go. It means more, somehow. Someday, once we have both met the graves not dug by our own hands my great grandchildren will find old notebooks in an attic and read about the allusive woman without a name. The woman who exuded brilliance and rustling leaves, who can only be done justice within art and they'll question and question and question. She loves her ancestors so much while I look more towards the descendants that will one day read my writing and hold on for another night because “if people like this girl existed, the world can’t be all bad”. She’s going to live forever now when a few months ago she didn’t want to live at all. I want my descendants to know about her and I can’t think of somebody more deserving of that.

If I asked her a year ago what some of her favourite things about this world were she would have likely remained silent. I remember seeing her tread water and sink below the fight with the currents from time to time. I remember her struggling and doing things she was ashamed of. Every mistake and transgression and fear of being alive. As somebody who spent years pouring my own self into the ocean I hope she knows that I understand. I understand her struggles and her previous flirtation with death. I understand it all and I hope she knows how much it meant to me when she saw me drowning and left the shoreline to remind me I’m not alone. I hope she knows that above all, I remember her through that. It’s hard to hate the world when people like her exist within it. Strong, resilient, beautiful people who inspire me to hold on for more sunsets. More sunrises. More warm hands and blue eyes and laughter.

I’ve been crying for a while because I asked her today what some of her favourite things about this world were and she answered.

I believe that speaks for itself.

Thank you for teaching me the true beauty of the colour orange. Above all, thank you for teaching me that the colour orange is just one out of six.

Untitled 17

To: The Girl Who Finds Beauty in Ordinary

The world is confusing and flawed and I'm sure you will change it in time. Breathe deeply. Time is an extraordinary thing. All the more curious when it is your own. You have spent your 18 years on this earth living as if every single day would be your last. From shedding tears over beautiful people and beautiful skylines, beautiful meals and beautiful knowledge your eyes have remained the same. Searching for the preceding adjective. Beauty. I've never met somebody quite like you and I doubt I ever will again. I'm thankful for that. You find beauty in the most ordinary things and I think that is what I admire most about you. The beauty of being could've been written by you with your eyes closed. Even when life is all pain, half corpse half weakly beating heart you still manage to tell me that it's beautiful. I am less than what I wish I could be but somehow you make me believe I am beautiful too. I don't think I've ever really thanked you for that. I smile because I know you are special, and because I know that I am special to you.

Breathe deeply. You are going to change the world somehow. Someday you will finally claim what you've worked toward for all of these years. Your painstaking efforts do not remain unnoticed by me. Eventually nothing will stand in your way. Breathe deeply. Trust me on this one. When I see a single sliver of sunlight hit floating dust motes just right, I think of you. When I share a smile with a customer at my minimum wage job, I think of you. When the cicadas sing in the dead of night, I think of you. You have helped me find the beauty in the simplest of things and pushed me towards the realization that life in itself is a miracle. Keep writing music. Keep writing poetry, although you don't call it that anymore. Keep loving. Keep smiling. Stay riveted. Time is an extraordinary thing and it is yours. Breathe deeply my love. You can't change the world overnight. Someday your name will be written in the stars next to various others that were put on - regardless of being too pure for - this earth.

To the girl who finds beauty in ordinary : you haven't changed the world just yet, but rest assured. You sure as hell changed mine.

Untitled 17

To : The Boy Who Taught Me Heartbreak (The Original ____)

We haven't spoken the way we used to in years but the warmth you used to provide has aged well. The promise I made to hate you forever after you broke my heart? All broken skin and runny nostalgia. I remember when we were 15 and I was "in love" with you. How we talked every night for years and walked around our survey long after the sun had closed her eyes. I remember every summer I spent trying to convince you that you were worthy of love. I can't help but hope you ended up believing it. Despite the pain my adolescent heart endured, I will always view you through a lens of unconditional love and admiration. Things ending differently isn't a thought I entertain anymore. Things are now, exactly as they should be. While the possibility of us meeting again in some run down coffeeshop is present, we will never again share the sugar-coated, innocent love we had when we were fourteen. I thought I would never get over that. But I have. And while it may have hurt for a very long time, I remain thankful. We were never bad people, just bad under those particular circumstances. It took a whole lot of experience and growth to realize this. My first love. My first heartbreak. Early and inevitable, but bittersweet nonetheless. Our late night FaceTime calls and 4 am hikes will live on in my memories forever. You may have caused pain, but overall you inspired growth. Through every loving phone call, hug exactly when I needed one, scribbled postcard (I still have every single one) and even the recent text message you sent to let me know you still admired me, makes me believe that I was lucky to have loved you to the extent that I did. Never hesitate to shoot me a text message or phone call. If you're sad again, or found happiness, or just want to catch up, I will always be there for you, as I know you are for me. Thank you for being kind and gentle with my naive versions of love. When I visit New York I will always chuckle to myself and think of you. Okay?

I'm just playing. Although those immature promises will always hold a special place in my heart. As will you. Forever.

That is one promise I know I will never break.

Untitled 17

To : The Girl Who Laid Beside Me When I Fell In Love With The Sun

We were in fact cut from the same cloth. You stated that in a note you left on my phone for me to read on my happiest and saddest days, and I do. I believe every word. Because when I look at you all I remember is the adrenaline rush of love and happiness I felt when I realized I had you back. When I realized that regardless of what the world threw our way, we were timeless. It was the best feeling in the world.

I hope you know that one day you will learn to forgive the world for how deeply it has hurt you. You are so kind and I don't think I will ever meet somebody as wise and loving as you. Summer nights were never just summer nights when you were there. I was watching you one day while you were trying to get a selfie of your eyes in the light. You were golden and glowing and covered in sun and it made my heart soar. Knowing, somehow, I got lucky enough to be placed in this life with you. I hope you know that whenever you're caught up in staring at the sky, everybody else is staring at you. It was you who was lying beside me when I fell in love with the sun. When I fell in love with the assurance that our friendship would remain strong even after it set. I feel at ease when I'm near you.

You acknowledge the pieces of me that I happen to like the most. You make me feel loved. You make me feel alive. You taught me that real friends still love you, even when they hate you. I just want you to know that you're beautiful, even on the mornings you can't leave your bed. I want you to know how much it means to me when you say you love me without even saying it. Through every "You can do this, I believe in you", "Have you eaten today?", "I said no because I didn't want to make you uncomfortable". Through every late night car ride, fingertip trailed down my arm, hand squeeze when you know I'm anxious, every time you've pushed me to do things I used to be afraid of, every little thing you do to ensure I exhale freely. You loved me just as well when I reached the mountaintop as you did when I hit rock bottom. You were one of the reasons I was able to rise from the bottom. That in itself has proven to me that you are my friend to the end. Bitch, we're really timeless. When I say I love you, you can be assured I'm not lying. Thank you for never silencing my toneless voice when I need to scream “Liv Bangers” into the sky. More importantly, thank you for singing along.

To the girl who laid beside me when I fell in love with the sun, sunshine somehow means more when you’re there next to me. I never knew I needed you until I found you. I need you. I love you. The world breathed a sigh of relief when we met. I think we’re a lot like those double layered songs we love so dearly. Offbeat and confusing until both layers finally sync up. You’re my best friend, so get used to being put first. You will always come first to me. Here’s to a timeless friendship.

Here’s to you, my best friend until the end.

Untitled 17

To : The Girl Who Shared My Most Innocent Years

I have a theory that growing up together has caused us to inherit the same brain. Seriously. It's unsettling how alike we think and act and speak together. You know that saying that goes "If you love something, let it go. If it comes back, it was always yours"? She was my something.

Thinking of you brings back all of my favourite memories. Between the cottages and campfires and your dangerous trampoline. Between french projects and burnt bagels and long nights. Stupid movies and cookies, laughing so hard we couldn't breathe. Back when everything was innocent. Back when things were fun and responsibilities were non existent and the only worry present was how we were going to convince our parents to let us see One Direction in concert. One night I remember the two of us lying outside on your trampoline drinking homemade lemonade and it was one of those moments. I call them my special moments because I feel like I'm the only one who notices them from within and I get to keep them. Just for me. The moments where I think to myself, damn. This life is really beautiful and this person is really wonderful and I am so happy. You have given me so many of those innocent (as well as not so innocent) moments.

Even when we coat our lungs with blue raspberry flavoured poison and scream throwbacks out the windows of our cars there is an unspoken promise to love each other the same way we did when we were children. So much has changed. We have both changed but the fact we found each other again gives me hope that maybe sometimes life works out exactly the way it should. It's in the way you sit next to me in silence on my worst nights. Your silence when I need it is enough for me to know that you love me too.

Thank you for always being there for me. Thank you for finding your way back into my life. I know sometimes I can be too close and too big and too much but thank you for choosing to welcome it. You are the funniest, most beautiful, resilient girl I have ever met. I'm sorry I don't tell you that enough.

Untitled 17

Thank you for sharing my most innocent years.

Thank you for growing up with me.

You will never quite understand exactly how much you mean to me. Nevertheless, I love you. Stay smiling. Forever.

Untitled 17

To : The Woman Who Gave Me This Life

In 2007 I wrote down in my journal that you were the strangest woman in the world. Mom, I know some of us are creatures of pattern and you are no different. I'm sorry I can't be more routine driven but that doesn't stop me from respecting the fact that you are. I like to think you raised me to be pretty observant and in stories I hear from my father I've come to notice that your proclamation is expressed in italicized font. *I have lived a pattern of pain.* Maybe your personal patterns are what you use to distract yourself from that. Distract yourself in order to stand straighter at work, at home, in life, whenever you need to. I fear that you think your definition of "success" is your only known route to survival. But you're not meant to survive. You're meant to live. My whole life I've been meaning to tell you that it's not always about where you want to end up. It's about where you are. It's about seeing and appreciating and thinking and feeling. Allow yourself to feel something every once in a while. I promise you it does not make you weak. I love you most in your late night baking and post work mental breakdowns. I love you most in your pajama pants and tears over my poetry. I love you most when you allow yourself to be human.

I know being my mother is far from easy but I also know there a lot more urgent things to be doing than rubbing my back after a hard day. Don't think I haven't looked at them from every comprehensible angle, and then some. Eventually you will find yourself empty on a day there is nothing left to do. Know that not every single one of your actions must add up to something. Don't feel guilty for needing a break every once in a while. You can't keep going without them. Take time to look back and realize that you don't have to move on and away from everything right away. You are a force to be reckoned with however there are some forces you need to first reckon within yourself. Sometimes there are no definitive answers. Sometimes there will be answers that you don't have. Sometimes you fail, but more often than not you don't. I know you find your fulfillment in success so remember that. A few failures are nothing compared to the world you have created for yourself. The world you have changed for everybody else.

Untitled 17

In 2018 I reread my journal and laughed out loud over "strangest woman in the world". When I was little I got A's and O's mixed up pretty frequently. You may be strange to me, but I love you for exactly who you are. Despite our fights and disagreements, it's clear that you have carried me for a lot longer than 9 months.

And for that, I agree with what my misspelling seven year old self meant.

You are the strongest woman in the world.

Untitled 17

To : The Man Who Gave Me This Life

I'm sorry for never calling enough.

I know that it probably feels like it's me failing to make an effort towards somebody who loves me unconditionally but please trust me. It's not. I do love you. I do miss you.

It just hurts because I can't help but see you the way I did as a child. As my hero. Taller than the old pine tree in the yard of the house I grew up in. Holding my hand and telling me that no matter how many times I couldn't jump in the swimming pool, you were still proud of me. I never did end up learning how to swim. I still know you cynical and drenched in cigarette smoke. Thinking yourself something death would never be able to touch. It's hard because a few months ago I was forced to start thinking about you as if you were already gone. Like my universe had already began to shrink in anticipation of your absence. I don't think I can say I'm sorry anymore than I already have. This grief is malignant as your honesty when you said "Bubbi, daddy's not going to be around forever".

I don't have the words to tell you that I never really believed any of this was true. Like somebody sick was just here pretending to be you. Taking things day by day the way I did as a child. Hoping you'd come home in time for Christmas. Ends up cancer is more than just a zodiac sign. Dad, we both know that grief this big can only take my words and tangle them until there is nothing left but silence. I'm sorry for the silence. I guess all that's left to say is I love you. Thank you for being my hero. I love you. I'm sorry. I love you.

It is thanks to you that I carry the name Bracci like a badge of honour. Knowing you are my father further solidifies my belief that I can achieve greatness someday. You are the most amazing man in the world.

Thank you for giving me this life, and above all, thank you for changing it.

Untitled 17

To : You

Although I dedicated an entire chapter to acknowledgements, I would still like to thank one incredibly important person. Without their presence, I would be nothing but an unread book on a shelf.

Thank you. Whoever you are.

You have read my words and explored the darkest and brightest creases of my heart. You have paid witness to the reality of my youth and subsequent catharsis. You have witnessed me blossom and grow as well as wilt and be trampled on. Now it is your turn. If you are cold, I wish you warmth and a pair of arms to teach you. If you are sad, I wish you happiness and people to share it with. If you are lost, I wish you guidance and a moment to catch your breath. I can only hope this book provided you with those things and much more. I am nothing without you. I am also nothing with you, however it feels a lot better to be nothing together. If you feel as if you are nothing remember that I am nothing too. You have read this book therefore I will always be with you. You are not alone. You never were.

I hope the world cuts you some slack, although it probably won't. So fight. Fight with every last breath because I am with you and I want you to fight. A friend once told me "Liv, the world is yours". And it is. It is yours. It is ours.

Thank you for reading this book. My book.

When I was 8 years old I wrote a letter to myself dreaming of having a book published by the time I turned 18. Through countless edits, deletions, mental breakdowns, and rearrangements, I did it. I wrote my first book. Without you, that little girl's wildest dreams would have never came true.

I will forever owe you all of the words.

Untitled 17

P.S. Congratulations little Liv. You did it kid.

92039981R00102

Made in the USA
Middletown, DE
05 October 2018